Enchanted World

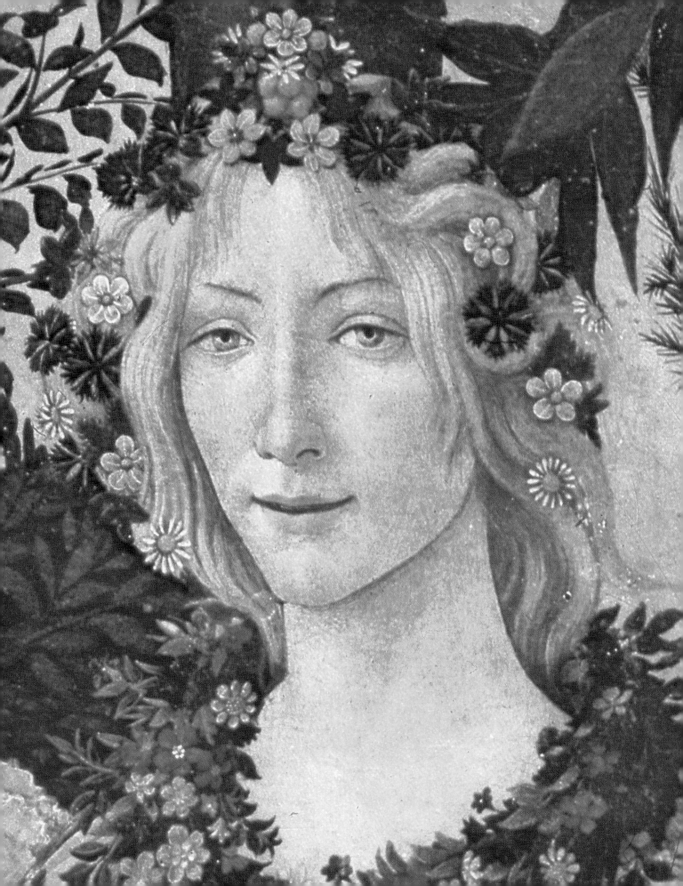

Bryan Holme

Enchanted World

The Magic of Pictures

With 96 illustrations, 44 in colour

Thames and Hudson

Spring (detail from *Primavera*). Sandro Botticelli. Italian, 1444–1510

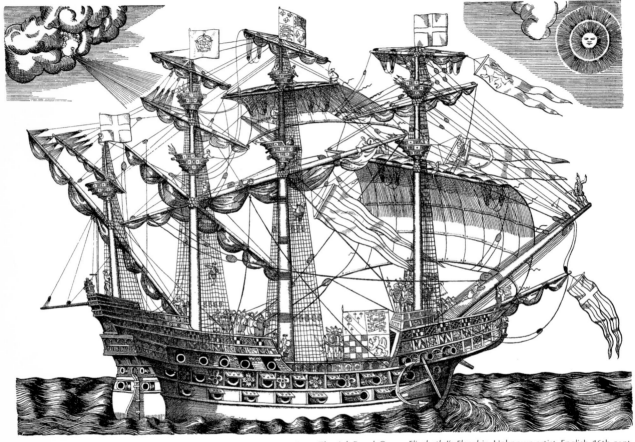

The Ark Royal, Queen Elizabeth I's Flagship. Unknown artist. English, 16th cent.

© 1979 Thames and Hudson Ltd, London

Filmset in Great Britain by Keyspools Ltd, Golborne, Lancs
Printed in Spain by Heraclio Fournier, S.A., Vitoria

Pictures are made for different reasons. Some instruct us about something: how to put a tent together, for instance, or how to fly a kite. Others, such as the ship on the opposite page, show *precisely* what a particular object looks like. Still others, as the rest of these pages show, are about life itself; people, animals, trees, flowers, and everything else that nature and the inventiveness of man has to offer . . . cities, circuses, boats, fireworks . . . anything you can think of. Once inspired by a subject, it is an artist's hope that he – and we – will be even *more* enchanted with the picture he finally develops out of it.

What makes one painting seem better than another is not always craftsmanship – this can result in a picture looking little different from a photograph – but when a certain magic guides an artist's eye and hand. Anyone who has ever tried to paint knows how a sweep of the brush you haven't thought about too much, if at all, will often give a picture more spirit and character than a dozen carefully applied lines or dots.

A certain magic lies in imagination too . . . ours as well as the artist's. We feel close to a picture when the subject is familiar and the way it is painted is the way we would love to have painted it if we could, but at other times how exciting it is to find an artist's flight of fancy carrying us, as if on a magic carpet, to an enchanted world we never imagined before.

So it is that pictures are made – and appeal to us – in various ways. We might love one painting because to our eyes at least, it is so beautiful, another because it is so true to life, or so amusing, or so fantastic, another simply because every time we look at it we have a happy feeling inside us. This of course is the most enchanting kind of all.

While the drawing opposite of the *Ark Royal* is purely factual, the idea of setting sail in Queen Elizabeth's flagship in the sixteenth century conjures up all sorts of romantic ideas about adventure and the sea. If no record had been made at that time, and if a present-day artist were asked to draw the *Ark Royal* from a written description, the problem he would have – especially with the rigging – would be immense. In fact he simply couldn't do it. As it is, the drawing is sufficiently clear for a new ship to be built almost exactly like it. This is the kind of picture that historians, artists and designers are always turning to for reference.

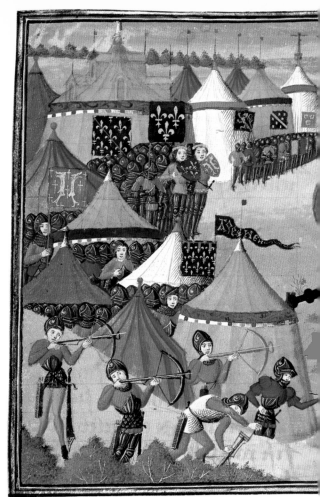

The Assault on the Strong Town of Afrique.
From manuscript of *Froissart's Chronicles*. French, 15th cent.

The Normans Building Ships for the
Invasion of England. French tapestry, 11th cent.

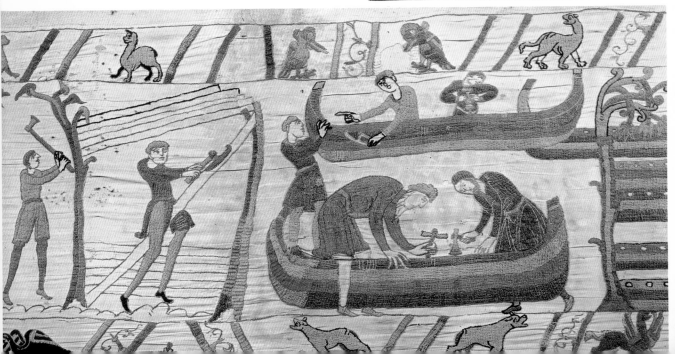

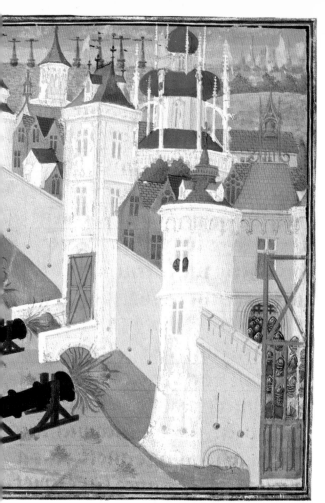

Before the camera was invented toward the middle of the nineteenth century, which in terms of world history was a very short time ago, coronations, celebrations, expeditions, battles and other events of topical interest were recorded by artists. That is, they had to be drawn or painted if anyone besides an actual eyewitness was to have any idea of the way everything and everyone looked.

If an artist wasn't actually present at the event, he would have to piece together scenes such as these, partly from what people who had been there told him and partly from his imagination or from studying the setting where the event took place, as well as the armour, weapons and other paraphernalia known to have been involved. At left, the artist almost certainly has made warfare look prettier than it was. Yet in the Middle Ages – according to written history, too – colour, pageantry and chivalry *were* the rule of the day.

The scenes below are taken from a two-hundred-and-three-foot long tapestry depicting in 'comic-strip' fashion the Norman invasion of England and the Battle of Hastings in 1066. The last stitch of wool in the linen was made about twelve years after that momentous day when William the Conqueror became King.

The Norman Invasion Fleet Crossing the Channel.

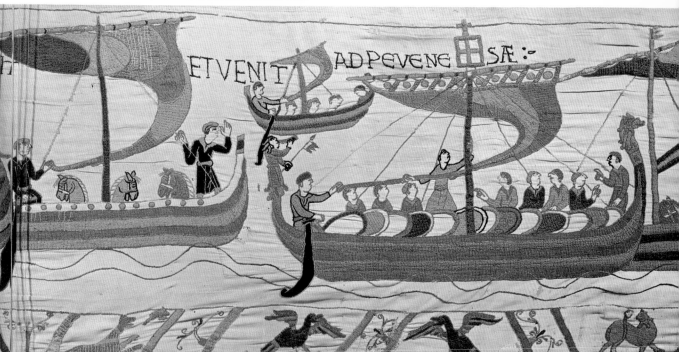

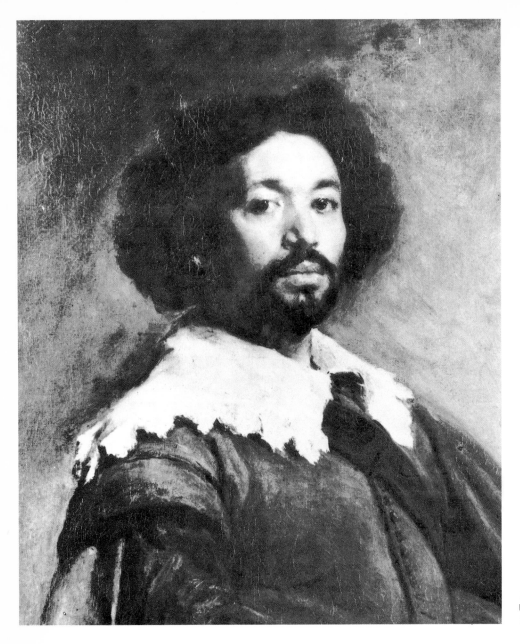

Princess of Saxony.
Lucas Cranach.
German, 1472–1553

Juan de Pareja. 1650
Diego Velázquez.
Spanish, 1599–1660

Artists have always been called upon to paint portraits.
This picture of a proud and handsome young Spaniard, attractive though it may be, is not all it seems. Juan de Pareja was born a slave, and remained one until his master, the painter Velázquez, set him free and made him his assistant. Juan de Pareja went on to become a well-known painter himself.

This girl also lived hundreds of years ago, and looks so natural, so familiar, so 'talkable to' that, except for her clothes, she might have been painted today. After the discovery of oil painting in the fifteenth century, artists were overjoyed with the three-dimensional effects that the oil medium suddenly had made possible. No photograph could be more realistic or do more justice to this charming princess.

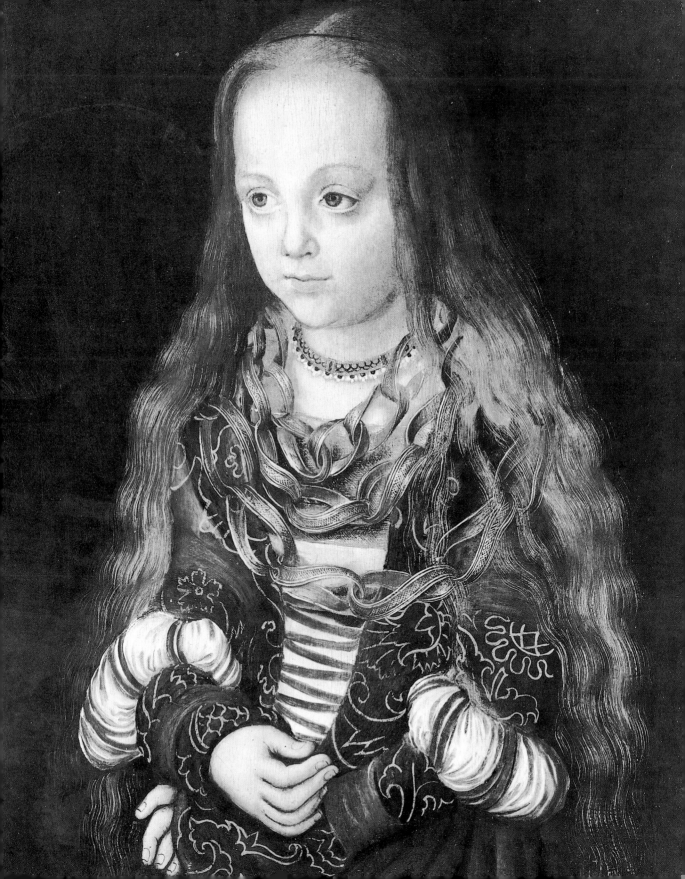

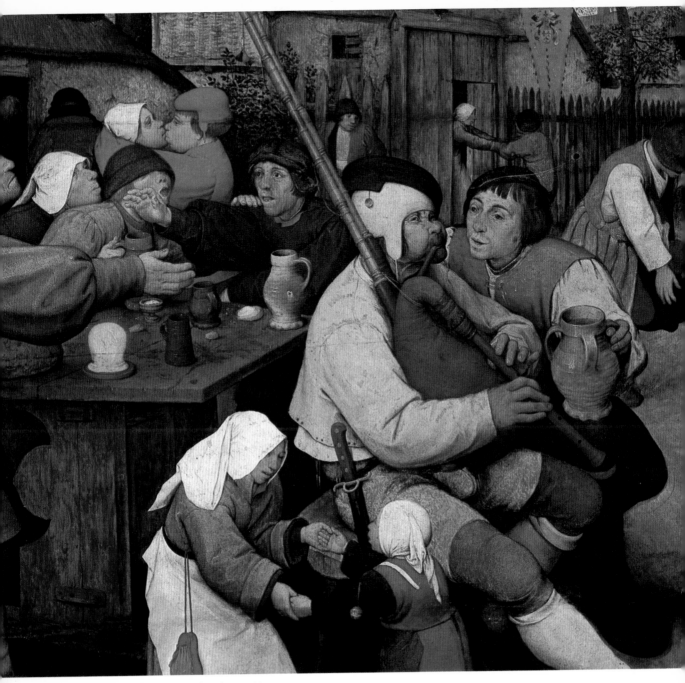

Peasant Dance (detail). Pieter Bruegel. Flemish, 1530–69

Familiar too are the faces of these country folk. And the dancing. One can all but hear the loud music of the bagpipe, the clumping of the dancers' feet, the quips and hearty

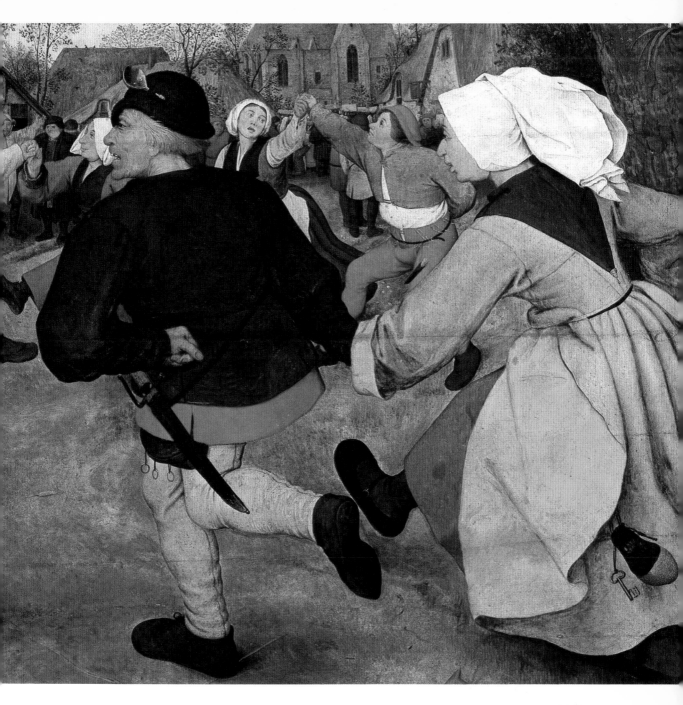

laughter of the merrymakers. Before Pieter Bruegel's day it was rare for an artist to paint a scene like this that no one had commissioned him to do for cash. Usually the Church, a king, a nobleman or merchant would order a scene or portrait to be painted to hang in a specific building – a place of worship, a palace, a town hall or mansion.

There were no museums to visit then, let alone art galleries in which an artist's work could be placed on exhibition and sold.

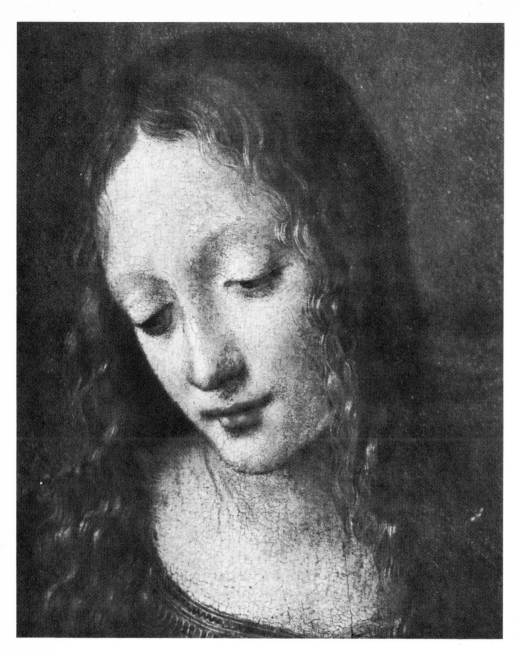

Adoration of the Shepherds
(detail). Pietro di Domenico.
Italian, 1457–1506(?)

Madonna of the Rocks
(detail). Leonardo da
Vinci. Italian,
1452–1519

After Rome became the centre of Christianity, the
Church became the chief patron of the arts. Throughout
the Middle Ages, particularly, it employed the very best
architects and artists to design and decorate the new
churches and cathedrals that blossomed throughout the
length and breadth of Europe.

Above is the lovely face of the Virgin Mary, taken from
one of Leonardo da Vinci's early masterpieces for an
altar; and at right is a detail from the Nativity by Pietro di
Domenico, with familiar scenes surrounding the birth of
Jesus. Behind Joseph and Mary are the animals in the
stable; in the distance the shepherds are dancing – more
gracefully than Bruegel's country folk – as a tiny angel
swoops down to tell the good news. On the road are
three kings or wise men who came from the East.

12

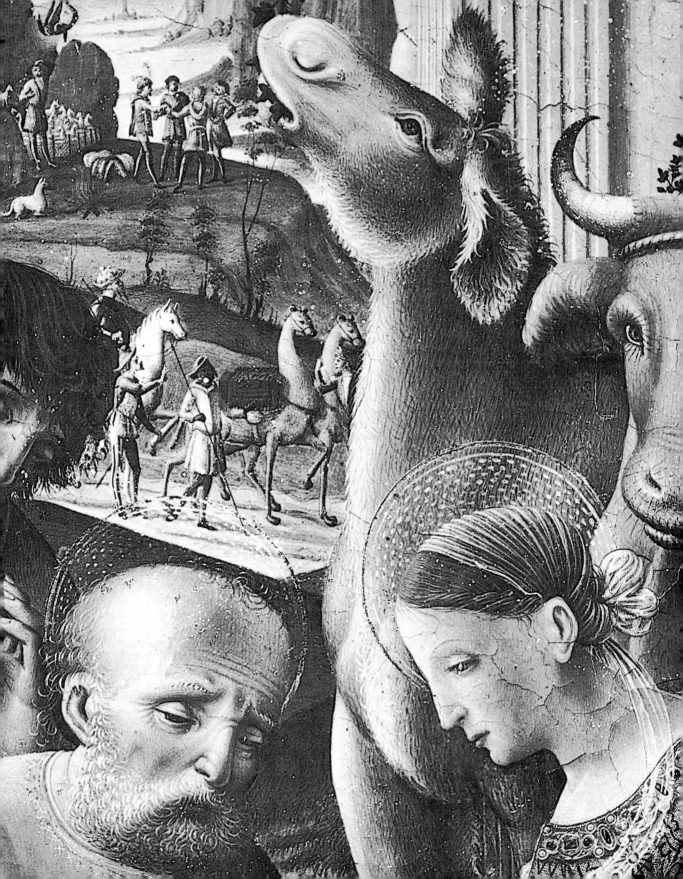

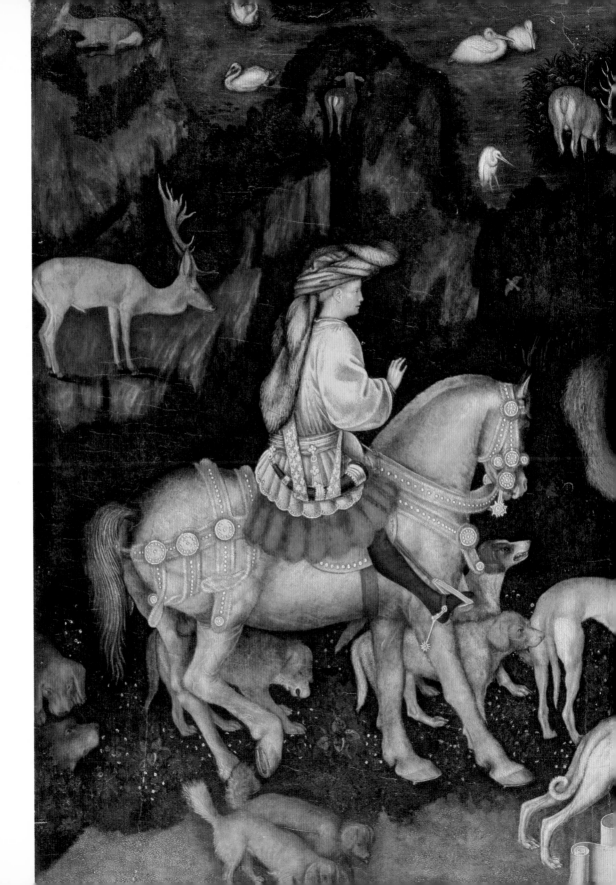

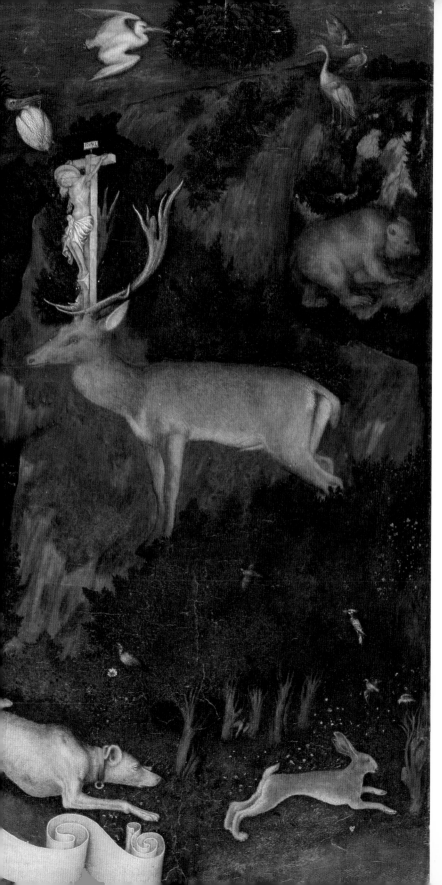

A striking painting by another fifteenth-century Italian. According to legend, a pagan soldier named Eustace was hunting in the forest one day when suddenly a stag turned and, lo and behold, there, between its antlers, Eustace saw a cross bearing the image of Christ. From that moment he was converted to Christianity. When the Roman Emperor Hadrian heard of this he was so enraged he gave orders for the soldier and his family to be bound and hurled to the lions. But, miraculously, not one of the hungry beasts in the den would so much as touch them.

Pisanello loved nature and drew animals so well that he chose the forest scene to paint. And, although he ignored perspective, how beautifully he executed every little detail.

The Vision of St Eustace. Pisanello (Antonio Pisano). Italian, 1395–1455

On the next page the artist Crivelli (unlike Pisanello) has made the most of perspective, so that our eye, after taking in the main figures, is gradually led on toward the distance. The detail of the angel's wing on page 16, a tiny portion of the picture shown in its entirety on page 17, demonstrates the love and care that went into painting the whole canvas.

It is interesting to see – as you can from the pictures in this book – how styles of painting – and popular subject mattter – have altered from century to century. As circumstances changed, so did the ways and speed with which artists worked. No one could produce a picture quite like this today, no matter how hard he tried.

The Annunciation, and detail. Carlo Crivelli. Italian, 1435–95

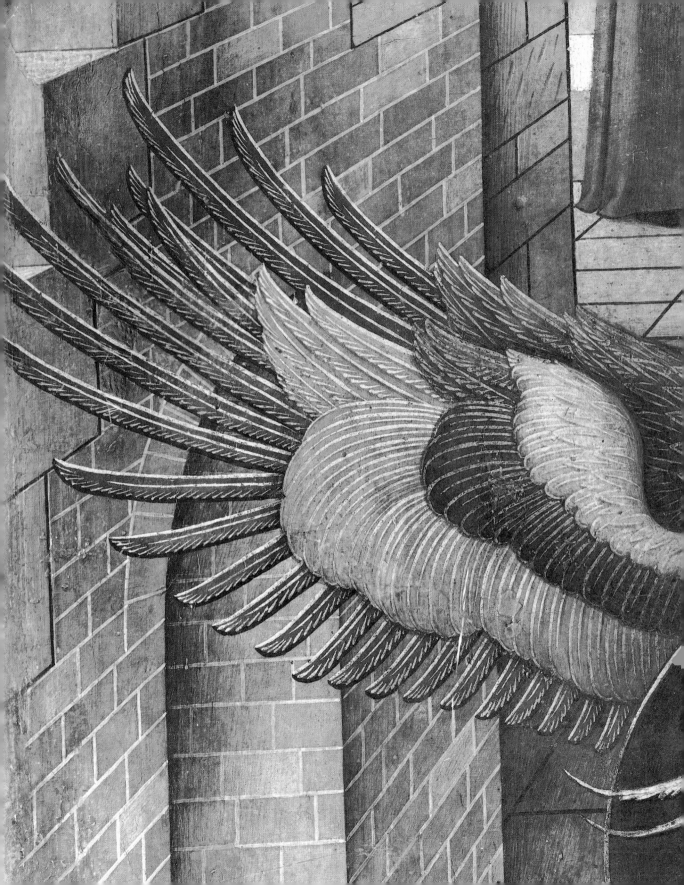

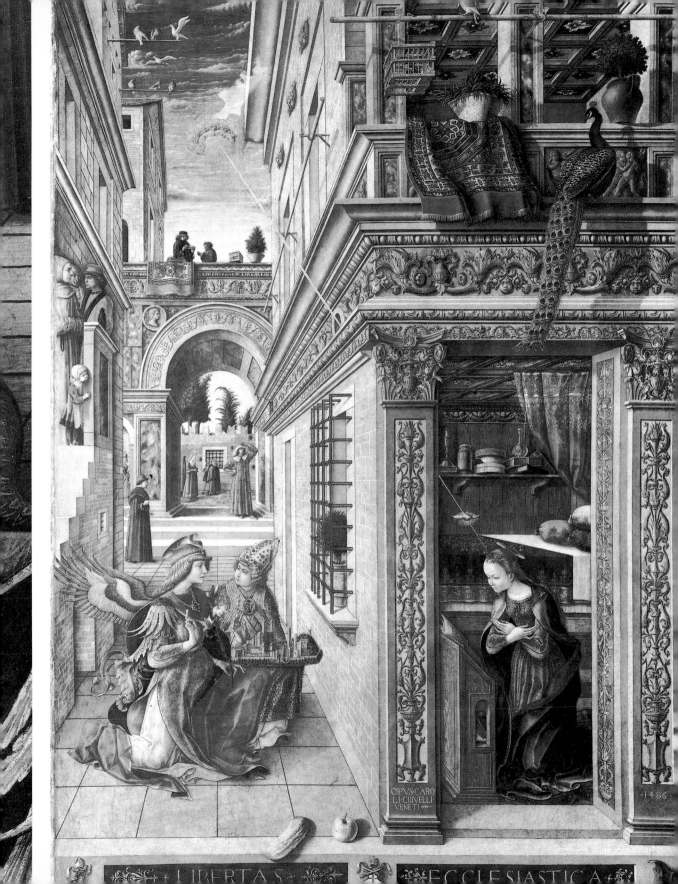

OPVS CARO
LI CRIVELLI
VENETI

·1486·

LIBERTAS · ECCLESIASTICA

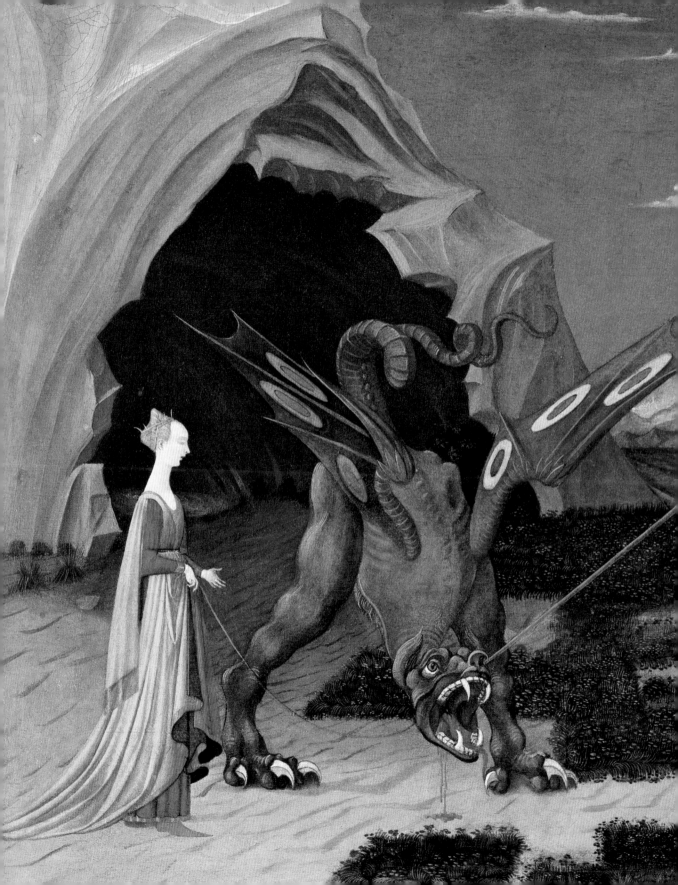

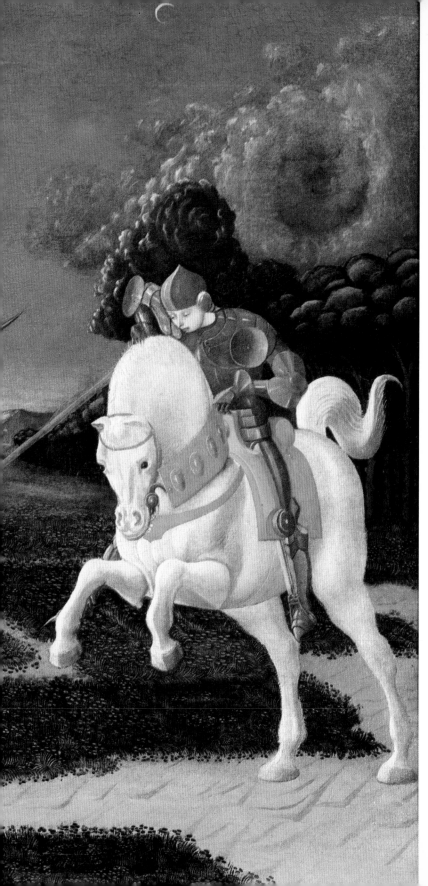

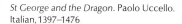

St George and the Dragon. Paolo Uccello.
Italian, 1397–1476

St George and the Dragon was an immensely popular subject with the old masters. As a real dragon was never around to oblige as a model, artists had a wonderful time imagining what one might look like, and competing with each other to create a monster that looked more fearful than anything anyone had dreamed up before. This is how an Italian artist saw England's patron saint at his moment of triumph. Ghastly though the face of the dragon looks, he has the most stylish wings – with rings.

19

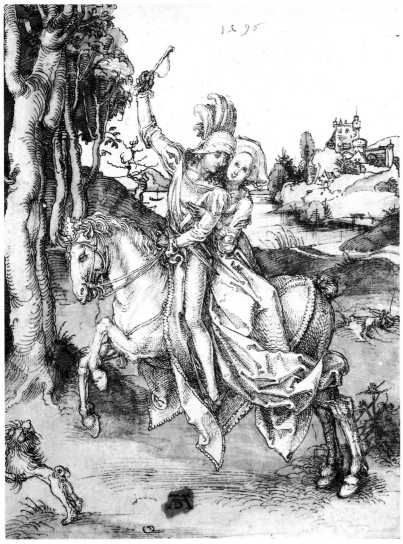

Lovers on Horseback. Albrecht Dürer. German, 1471–1520

Here we are treated to a much more light-hearted kind of enchantment. The watercolour looks like an illustration for a fairy tale, but it isn't. The fifteenth-century artist, Albrecht Dürer, chose to paint a romantic young couple of his day on horseback – as a similar couple today might be seen out riding on a motorcycle.

Another fifteenth-century rider, also looking like the hero of a fairy tale, is Lorenzo de' Medici on the opposite page. In his day he did more to further the fantastic revival of art and learning – known as the Italian Renaissance – than any other ruler of Florence. They called him Lorenzo the Magnificent.

Lorenzo the Magnificent as One of the Three Magi. Benozzo Gozzoli. Italian, 1420–95

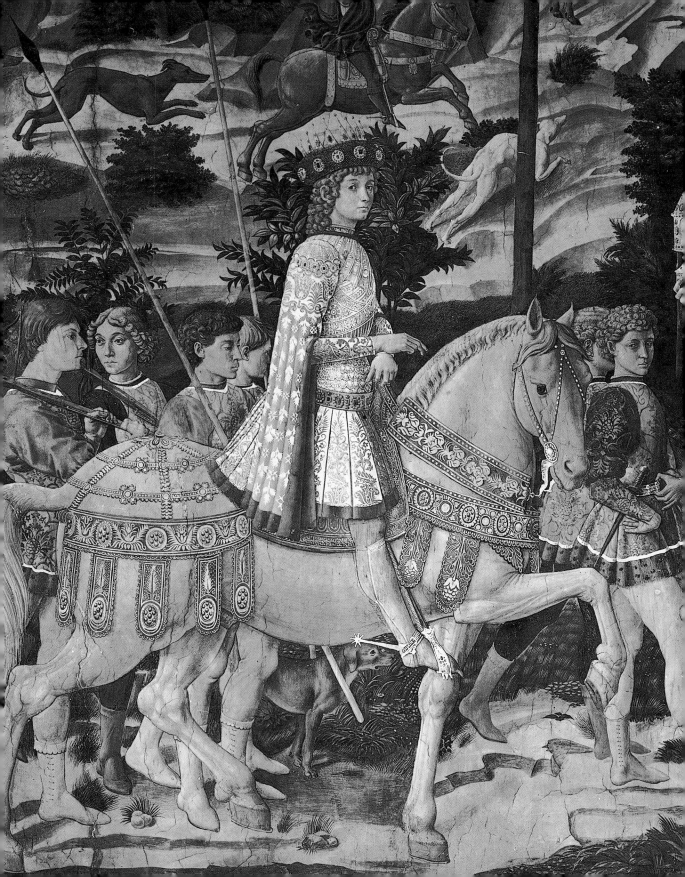

Fairyland's equivalent of the guardian angel is the fairy godmother who, like Cinderella's or the Sleeping Beauty's, could bring all sorts of magic to pass with the wave of her hand or the touch of a wand.

Woodcut from *Popular Tales of Olden Time.* Unknown artist. English, c.1840

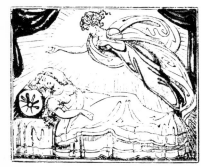

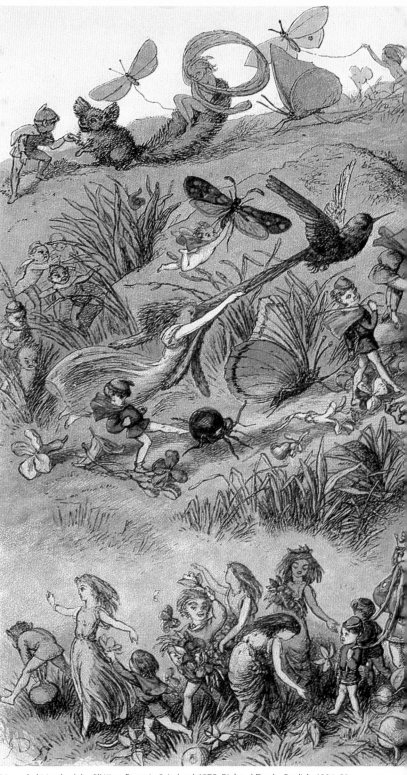

A lively procession of fairies, elves, birds, snails, butterflies and other fairyland creatures. The idea was real enough in the artist's mind for him to paint this fanciful scene in convincing detail and with altogether enchanting results.

Triumphal March of the Elf King. From *In Fairyland*, 1875. Richard Doyle. English, 1824–83

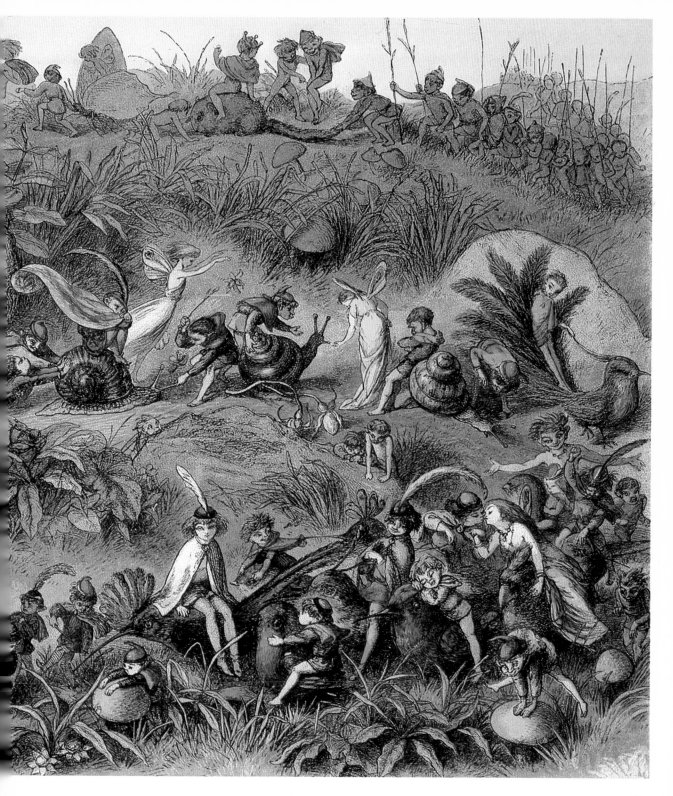

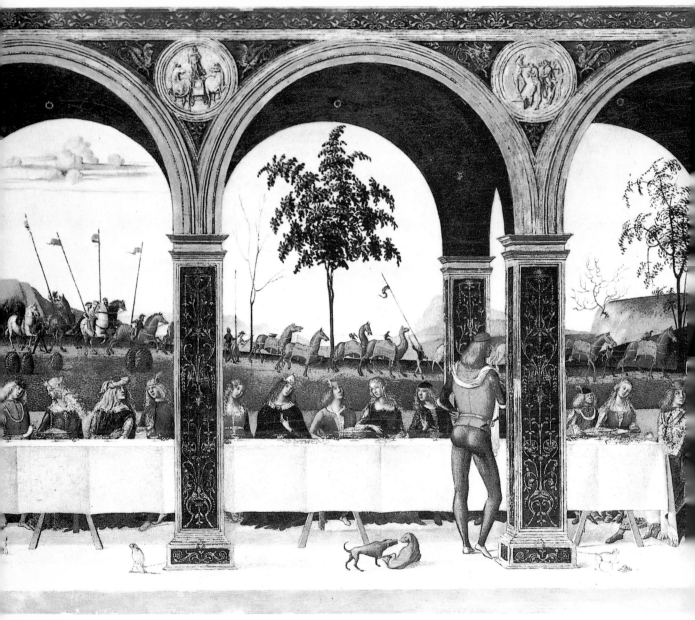

The Story of Patient Griselda. Master of the Story of Griselda. Italian, active c.1500

The elegant banquet was painted by a fifteenth-century Italian Renaissance artist, and the famous fairy tale scene at right, showing Beauty at dinner with the Beast who begs her to marry him, is by a nineteenth-century English lady who, like other artists of her day, was greatly influenced by the Renaissance painters.

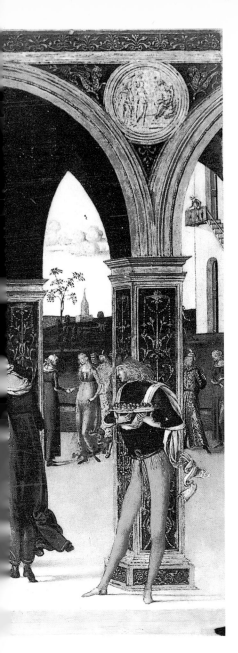

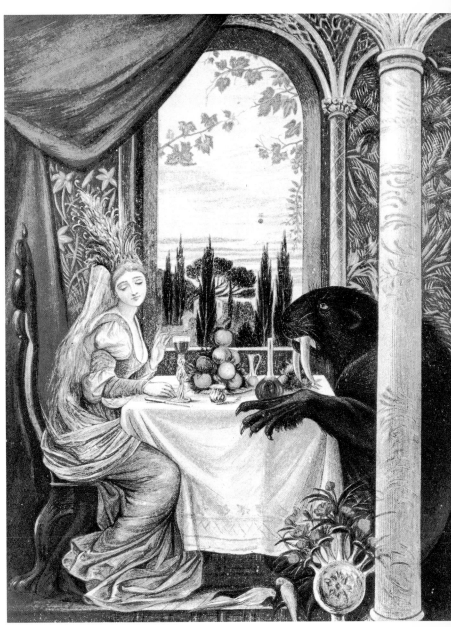

Beauty and the Beast. From *Beauty and the Beast*, 1875. Eleanor Vere Boyle. English, 1825–1916

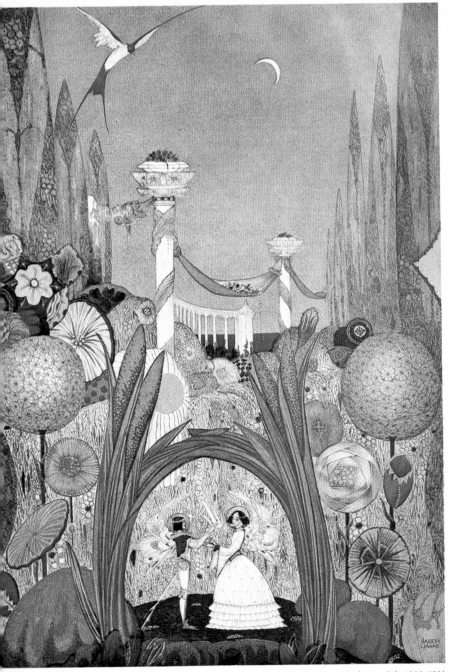

Thumbelina. From Hans Christian Andersen: *Fairy Tales*, 1931. Harry Clarke. English, 1890–1931

The reason that each of us may like the paintings of one artist better than those of another is because all of us see things as differently as the artists themselves do. Here is the way two different artists saw Thumbelina, the tiny heroine of Hans Andersen's fairy tale who, at the end of the story, was flown by the friendly swallow to a sunny island in the south. There Thumbelina met and married a prince her own size, who gave her a pair of wings to match his, so that from that day on the two could fly off together wherever they wished.

Thumbelina. From *Andersen's Fairy Tales*, 1882. Eleanor Vere Boyle. English, 1825–1916

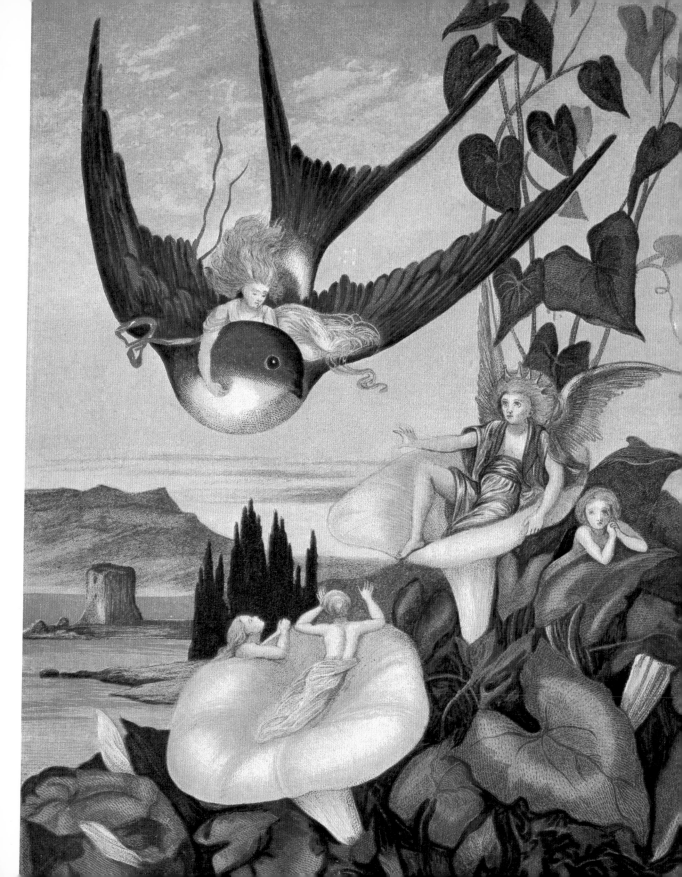

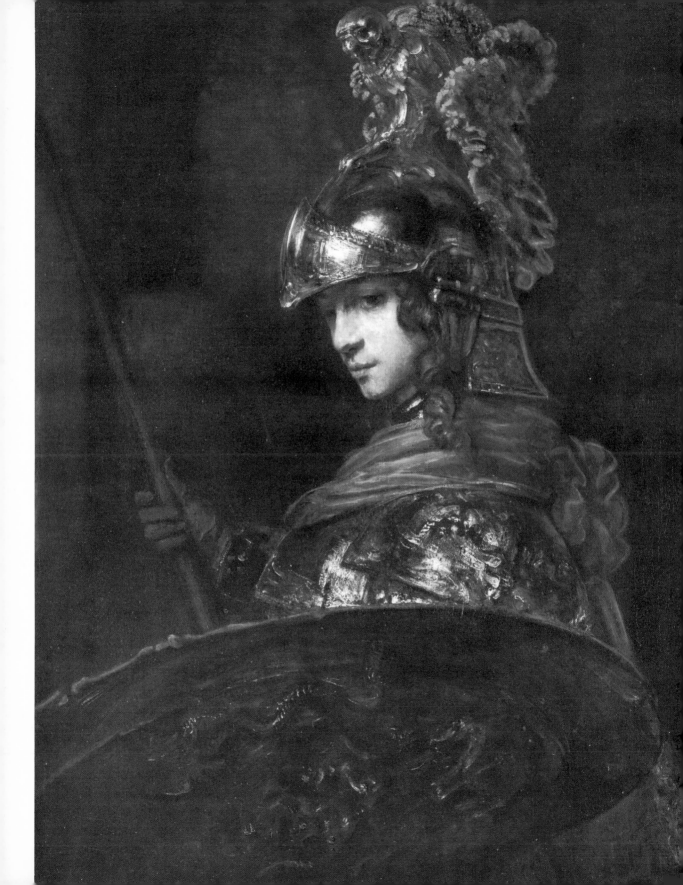

It is to the ancient Greeks that western civilization owes many of its legends, particularly the tales of gods and heroes. Opposite is how the Dutch painter Rembrandt envisioned Pallas Athena, the goddess who stood for beauty and strength and wisdom. Her temple was the Parthenon, remains of which still stand on the Acropolis to the wonder and delight of the millions of visitors who still flock to Athens every year and dream of the past.

The Embarkation of St Ursula. Claude Lorrain (Claude Gellée), French, 1600–82

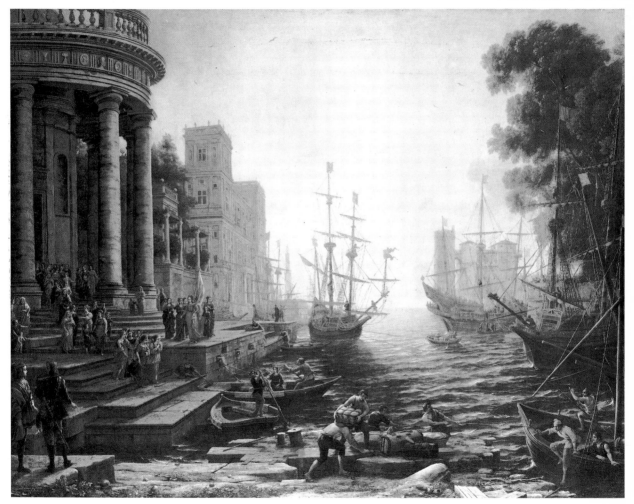

Pallas Athena.
Rembrandt van Rijn.
Dutch, 1606–69

Painting scenes from legends, such as the one above from the Christian story of St Ursula, provided romantically inclined artists with the opportunity of showing just how beautiful a landscape or a city or a port *could* be. It takes a moment before we find the heroine of the story. Follow the movement of the people along the quay down the steps, and there she is: Princess Ursula of Brittany, with her girl attendants, off on a pilgrimage to Rome.

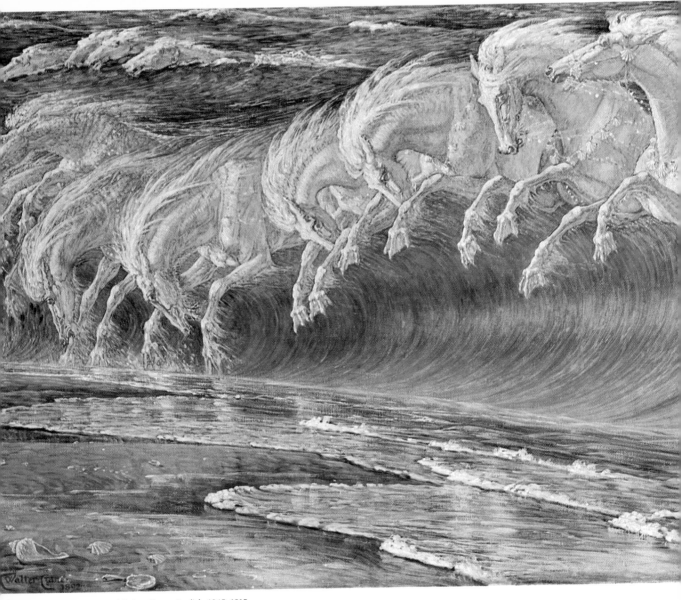

Neptune's Horses. Walter Crane. English, 1845–1915

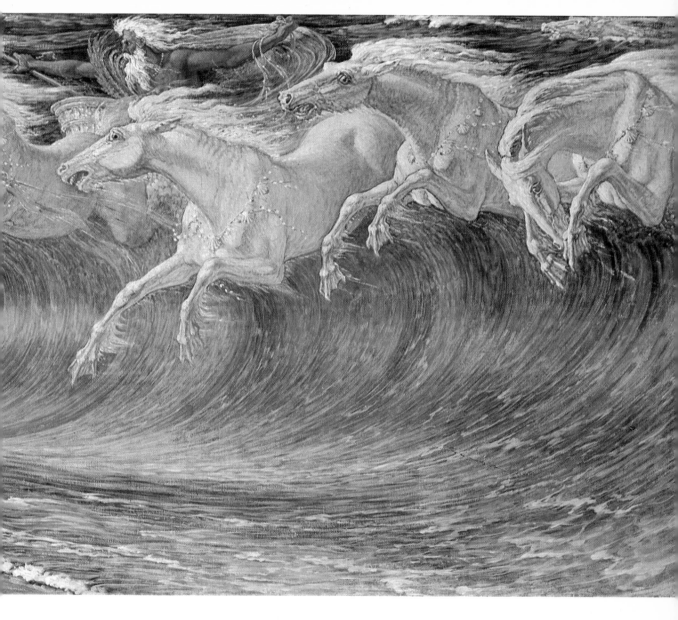

Many legends have grown out of daydreams and make-believe. Along the beach, how often the crests of waves suggest flowing white manes – as Neptune's horses are always supposed to have. This painting of the God of the Sea riding ashore in his chariot created a sensation when it was first seen in Paris in 1889. Symbolist art, as this type of picture soon came to be called, was a reaction against ordinary studies of everyday things. Gods, heroes, and the mysteries of the universe seemed much more exciting to the younger generation than, for instance, a still-life study of a bowl of fruit or flowers, a glimpse of the countryside, or a typical city street.

31

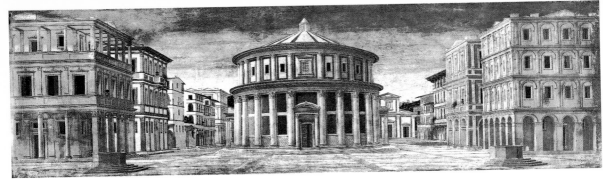

An Ideal City. Piero della Francesca. Italian, c.1410–92

On this page we see quite the opposite of a typical city street. Above is how one fifteenth-century Italian artist envisioned an ideal city, and below is how another one chose examples of his favourite forms of architecture and grouped these buildings around an imaginary city square.

At right the modern Spanish master Salvador Dalí has also used architecture, but to create an altogether different kind of fantasy. Perhaps in the man's dreams the tower bell suddenly came alive as a girl with a skipping rope? The more mysterious a painting, the more fascinating it is because we can go on interpreting its meaning in any way we choose. This is particularly true of dream-world (or so-called 'Surrealist') painting, of which Dalí has remained the most famous exponent in our century.

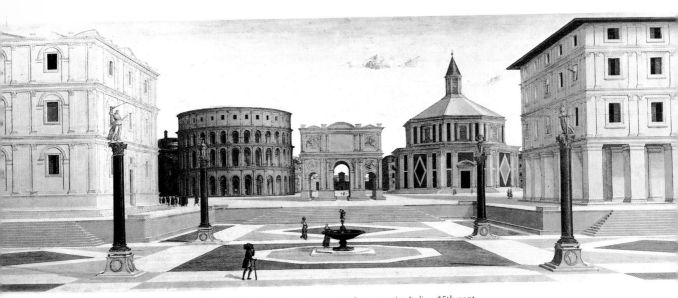

Architectural Perspective. Unknown artist. Italian, 15th cent.

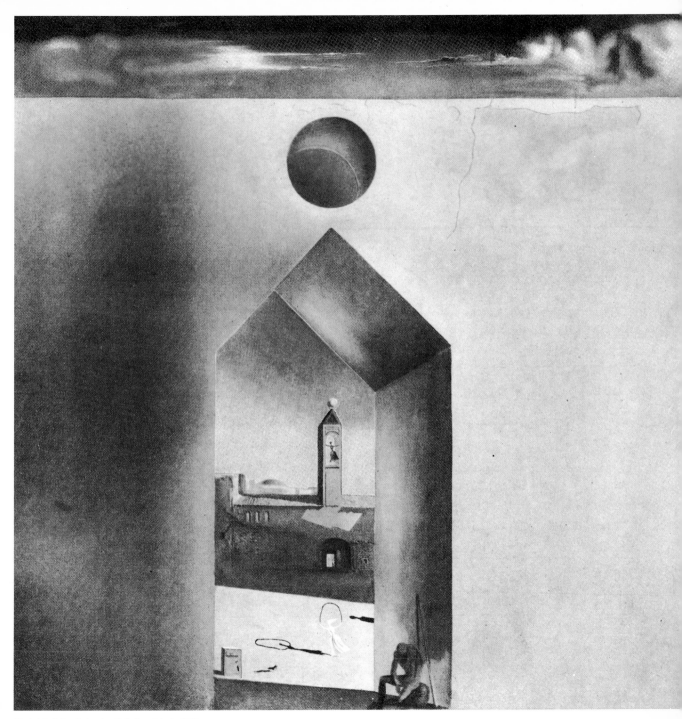

Nostalgic Echo. Salvador Dali. Spanish, b. 1903

The Effects of Good Government.
Ambrogio Lorenzetti. Italian, 1265–1348

Here the local government
commissioned Lorenzetti to paint
scenes that would show how happy
and contented everyone who lived
in fourteenth-century Siena was.
Besides the group of women

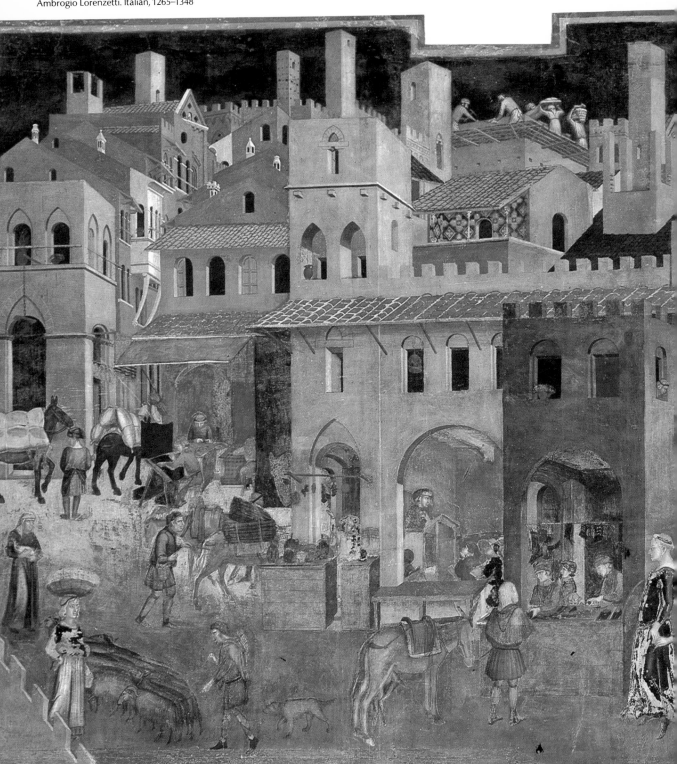

dancing, the scenes through the windows of the shops and the school, and the busy builders working on the roof, there is the beauty of the medieval Italian city itself with its white walls, pink roofs, and tile balconies all the way up the narrow winding street.

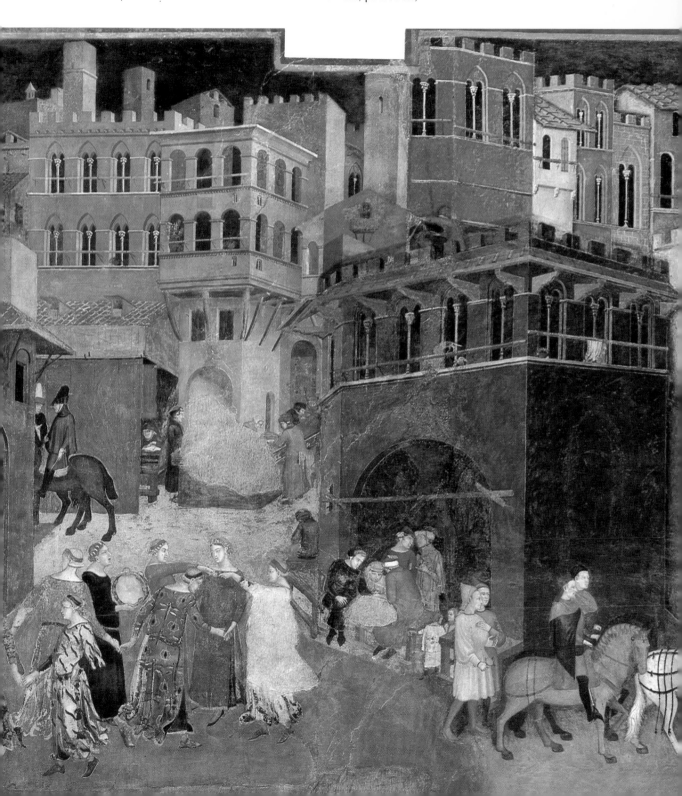

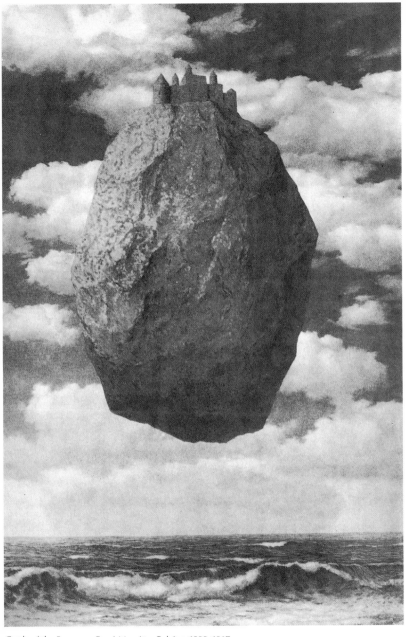

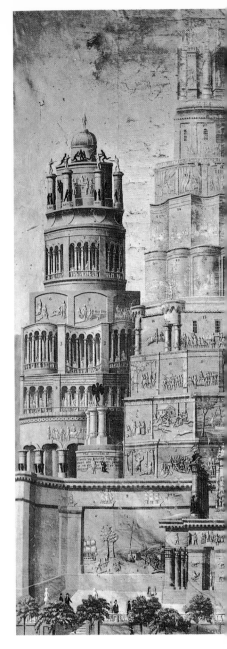

Castle of the Pyrenees. René Magritte. Belgian, 1898–1967

By painting a castle in the air as realistically as if it had been photographed, the Surrealist artist Magritte has cleverly made the impossible look possible. This is the sort of picture that immediately attracts attention, that people can't help talking about and returning to look at again and again.

The painting at right represents an American artist's dream city long before any skyscraper was built.

Sometimes dreams produce entertaining flights of the imagination; occasionally, too, they suggest something that in the end can turn out to be perfectly practical – like skyscrapers.

36

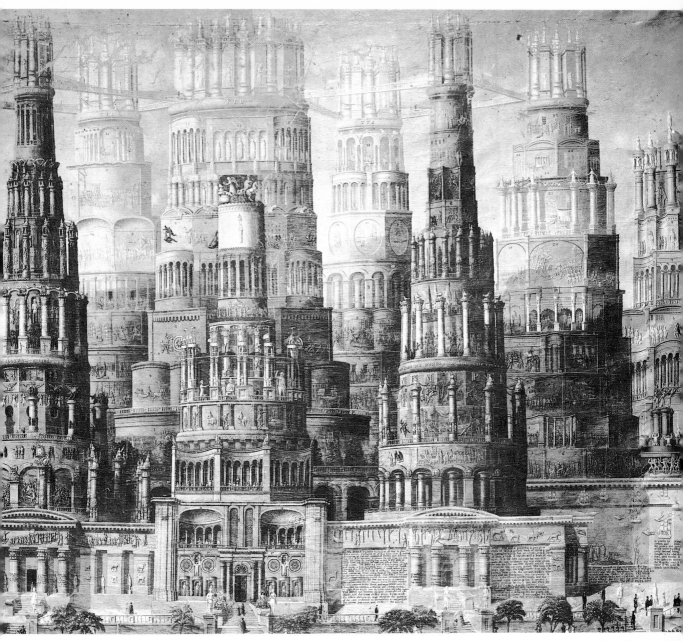

Historical Monument of the American Republic. Erastus Salisbury Field. American, 1805–1900

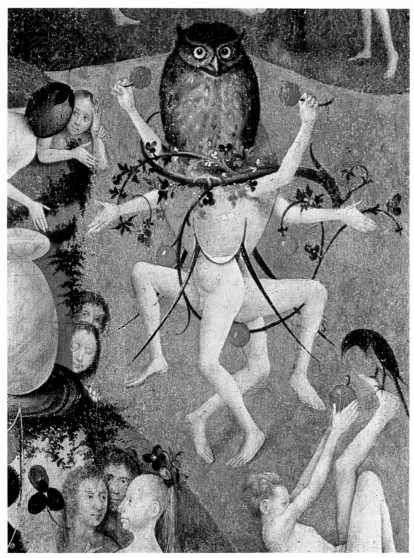

Garden of Delights (details). Hieronymus Bosch. Dutch, c.1450–1516

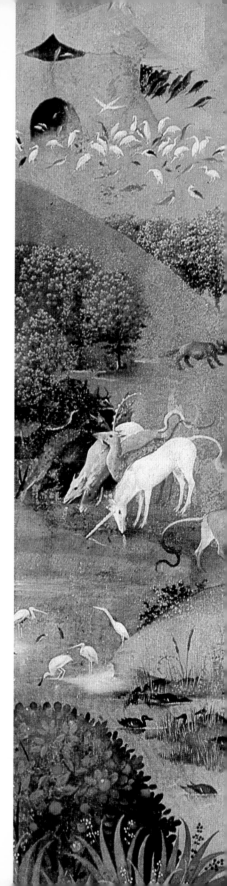

One of the great artists and dreamers of all time was Hieronymus Bosch. Probably he was better than anyone at making dreams seem real. Both pictures here are details from the same large painting of the Garden of Delights.

The fountain, surrounded by an elephant, a giraffe, and other wild animals, is as fanciful as anyone is likely to imagine, but the surprising detail above is more typical of the weird kind of riddle Bosch loved to use to tease our eyes and minds.

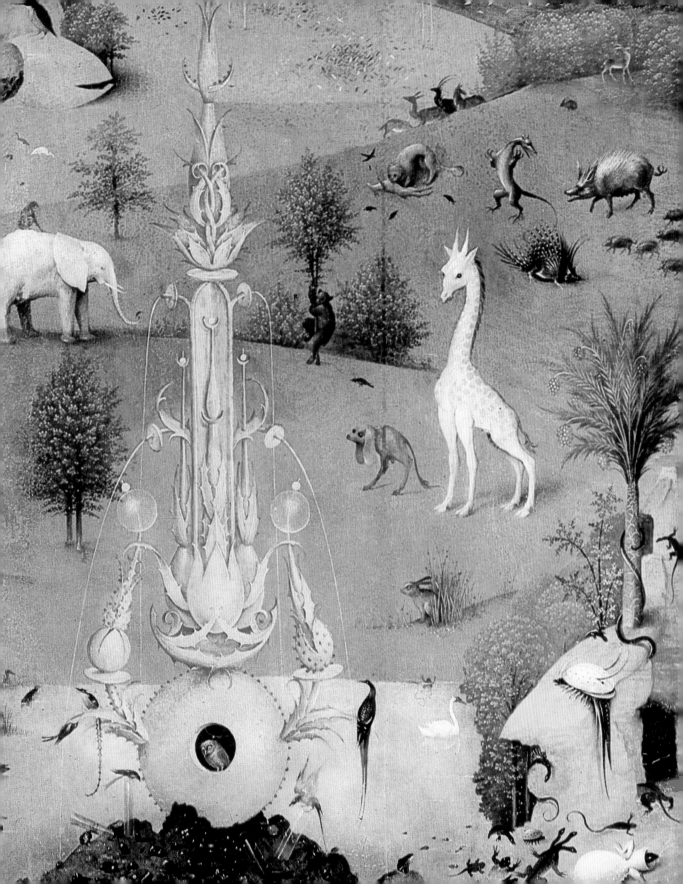

The Dream. Henri Rousseau. French, 1844–1910

Rousseau's mysterious jungle isn't as well painted as Bosch's Garden of Delights. Not nearly. The artist, a customs man, taught himself how to paint, but his imagination (he never saw a jungle in his life) and the spirit and colour with which he enlivened his pictures more than make up for the shortcomings in technique. When Rousseau painted *The Dream* in France in 1910 it wasn't the fashion to admire so-called primitive pictures or folk art like this. But Rousseau changed all that.

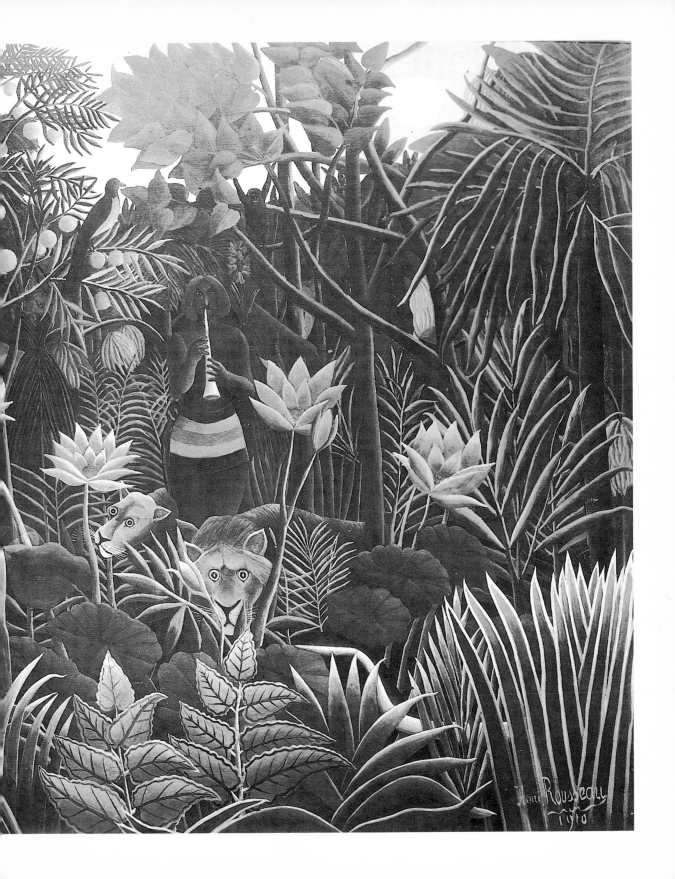

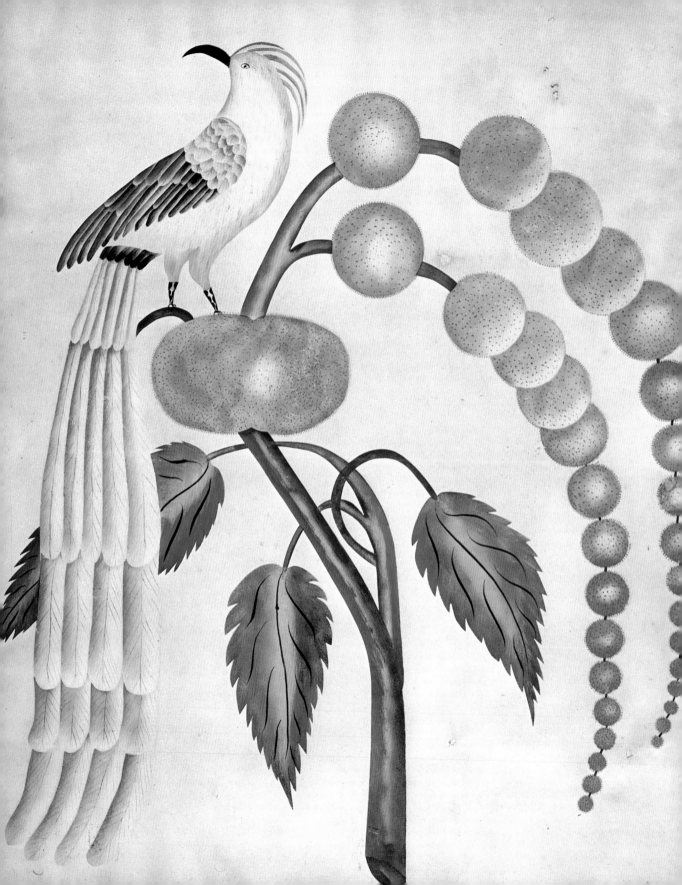

Tropical Bird with Fruit. Unknown artist. American, 19th cent.

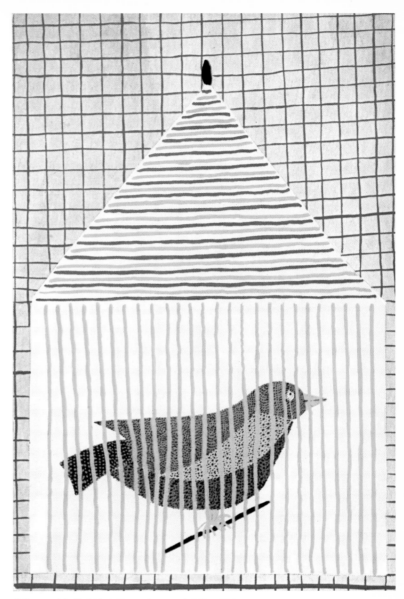

A Cage and its Bird. Maria Teresa Lazzaroni. Italian, 20th cent.

Simpler, but in its own way just as colourful and charming as Rousseau's painting on the previous page, is the decorative watercolour (opposite) by an American folk artist. She too composed the picture in her mind, rather than painting it from life. With the use of stencils she arranged the heavy trailing stems of fruit, the leaves, and probably the bird's tail also, before she completed the picture with freehand strokes of the brush.

A girl of fourteen saw and painted a caged bird this way. What prompted her to add the extra squares around the cage even she might be unable to remember or explain. And there would be no reason to. In art anyone can do anything that he sees as suitable, particularly if the result is as pleasing as this.

43

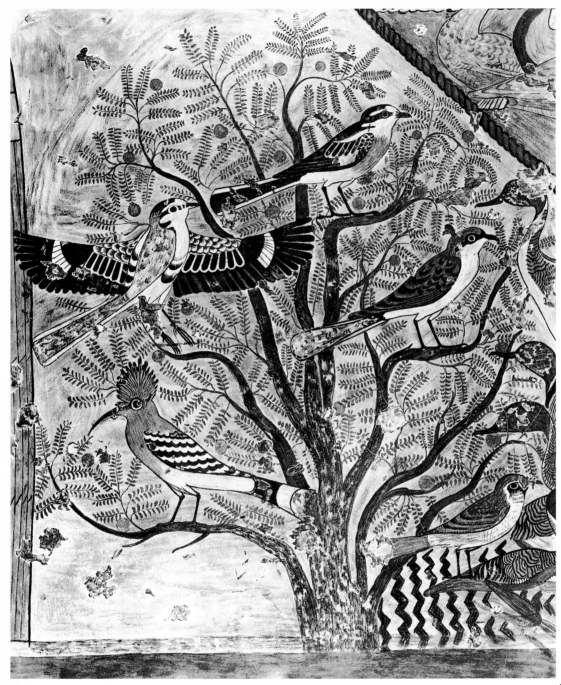

Birds in Acacia Tree. Unknown artist. Egyptian, c. 1900 BC

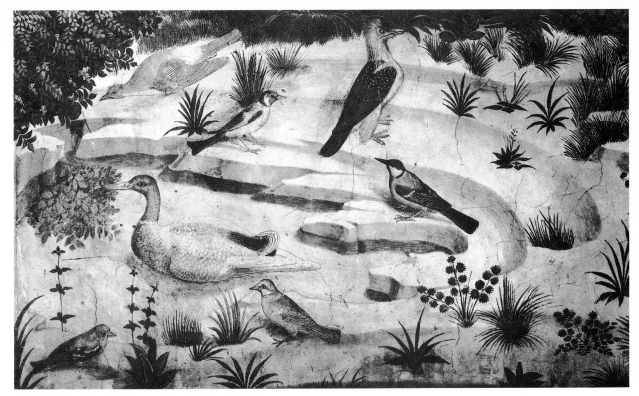

Birds (detail from *Paradise*). Benozzo Gozzoli. Italian, 1420–95

Five more representations of birds, each done in a
different century in a different country and with different
materials or implements. Obviously birds haven't
changed through the centuries, nor have the different
ways people have seen and, for the most part, depicted
them. Almost any of these particular examples could just
as well have been done by an artist living today as
yesterday . . . or tomorrow.

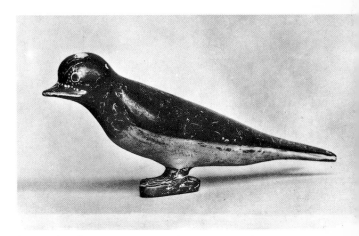

Scent Bottle in the Form of a Swallow. Unknown artist. Greek, c. 600 BC

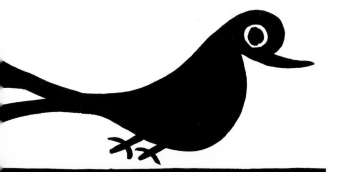

Zuñi Pottery Design: Bird Motif. Unknown
artist. American Indian

45

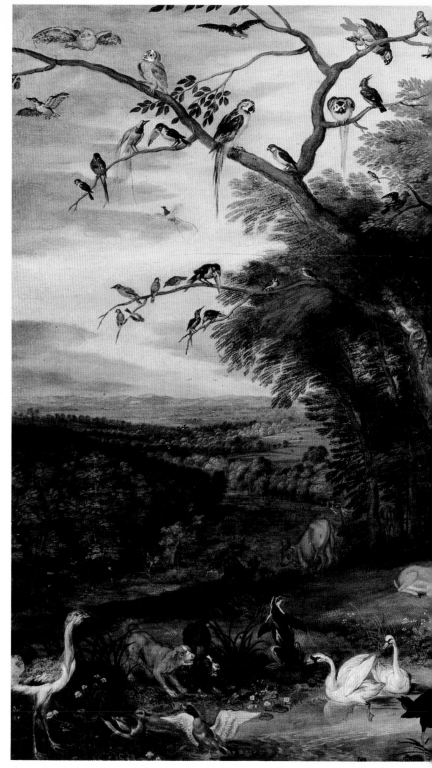

Here is how Jan Bruegel envisioned the Garden of Eden, with pairs of animals living in perfect harmony, one with the other. The scene is as gentle and sweet as Bosch's Garden (on pages 38–39) is wild and fanciful. Obviously Bruegel was more interested in the animals than he was in Adam and Eve, whom he made very small and placed in the distance – off there to the right. Incidentally, it was Jan Bruegel's father, Pieter, who painted those lively Flemish dancers back on page 10.

The Garden of Eden. Jan Bruegel. Flemish, 1568–1625

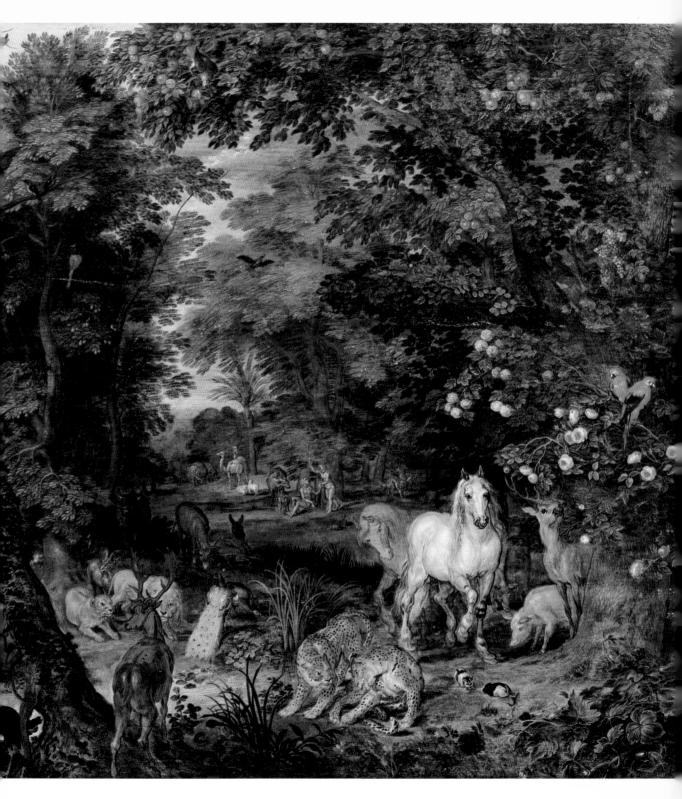

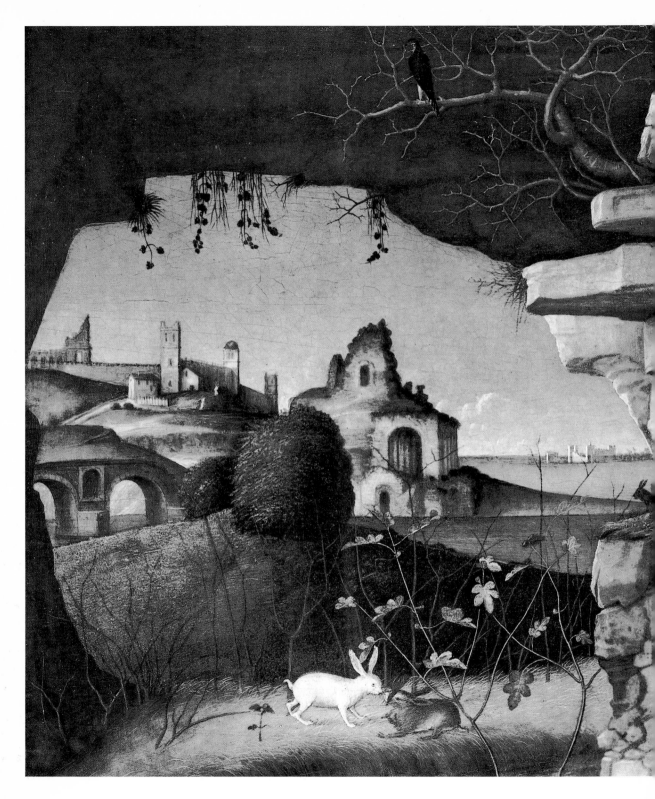

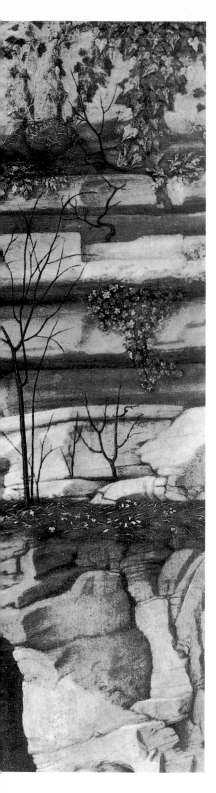

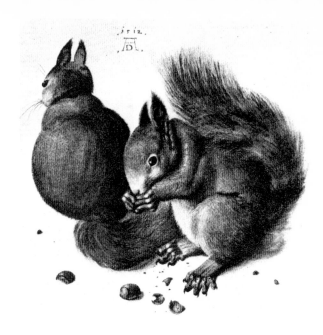

Old master paintings are often so large and detailed that a small background scene like this is easy to miss. If we turned back to Jan Bruegel's picture of Eden, chances are that another bird or animal might *seem* to have crept in since we last looked.

Sometimes rediscovering a favourite picture is as rewarding as discovering a new one. Dürer's squirrels must be the most famous in the world.

The drawing below was not originally intended to hang as a picture on a wall, but merely to show nature lovers what a black-tailed hare looked like. It is one of thousands of records the pioneering artist, Audubon, made of the animals and birds of North America.

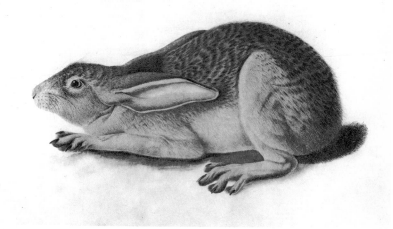

No animals are blue, but thousands of years ago an imaginative potter decided to create a tiny hippo and make him as cheerful looking as the bluest of Egyptian skies. Originally placed in a Pharaoh's tomb to help keep the spirits of the dead happy, 'William' now resides in a large museum where his more joyful task is to keep the spirits of the *living* happy. It's an interesting thought that had this most famous of all little hippos been plain and grey like a real one, not much attention would have been paid him at all.

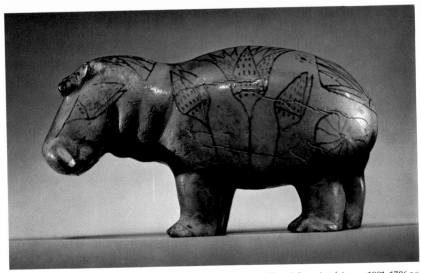

Hippopotamus ('William'). Egyptian faience, 1991–1786 BC

Cow. Pottery, style of 18th cent.

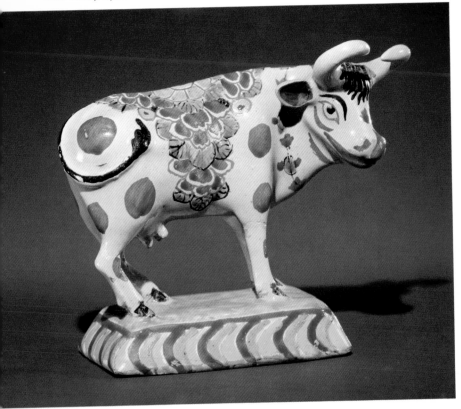

Below is another example of what imagination, colour, and a sense of humour can do. Few people can look at the gaily decorated cow without returning that smile. Designers always like to point out that no reproduction can copy nature *exactly*, therefore why not go to the opposite extreme and paint flower upon flower on a cow, if that's what your fancy dictates?

The scene opposite, from an old Persian manuscript, also uses flowers in a stylized, decorative way. The elegant horses, their owners, the landscapes; everything comes together in a closely knit pattern which suggests a fairy-tale land of long ago. In Islamic paintings like this it is said that the absence of shadows is because the story takes place in a higher world where legends are true.

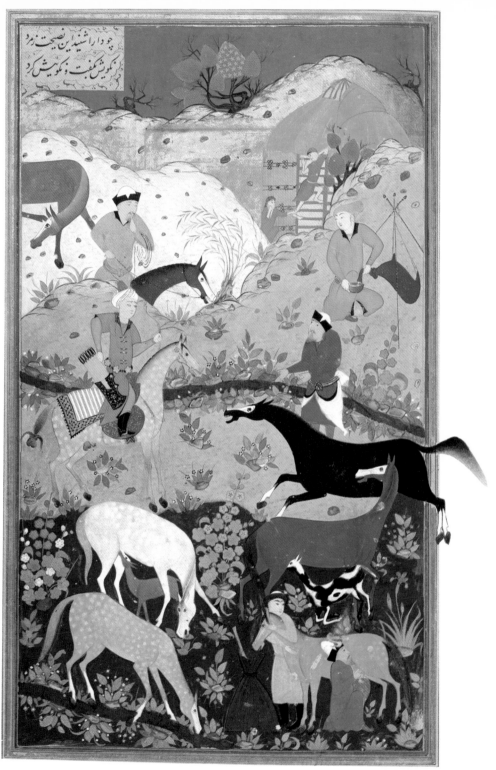

King Darius and Herdsman. From manuscript of Saidi: *Bustan*, 1522–3. Persian, 16th cent.

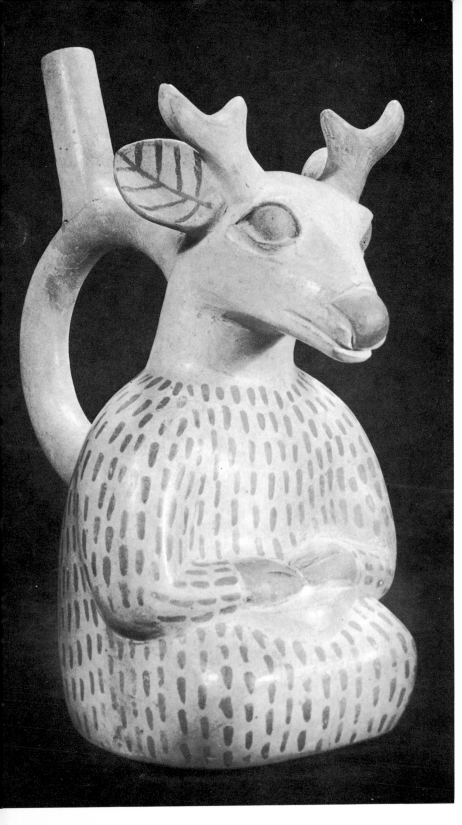

A Peruvian potter designed the top of this jug in the shape of a deer and with a mouth that conveniently serves as a spout. But look at the lower half of the jug: is this really a seated deer, or is it a human with arms folded and legs tightly tucked up under a spotted gown? Some have said that the jug reminds them a little of what happened to Bottom in *A Midsummer Night's Dream*.

Stirrup-spout Pottery Vessel in Form of a Seated Deer. North Peru, Mochica style

How different the painted deer on the opposite page are. With sharp clear strokes of a watercolour brush the Japanese artist made these beautiful animals as natural looking as he possibly could. Nothing distracts our eyes from the charming trio except for the big surprise – a bat overhead.

Deer and Bat. Shibata Zeshin. Japanese, 1807–91

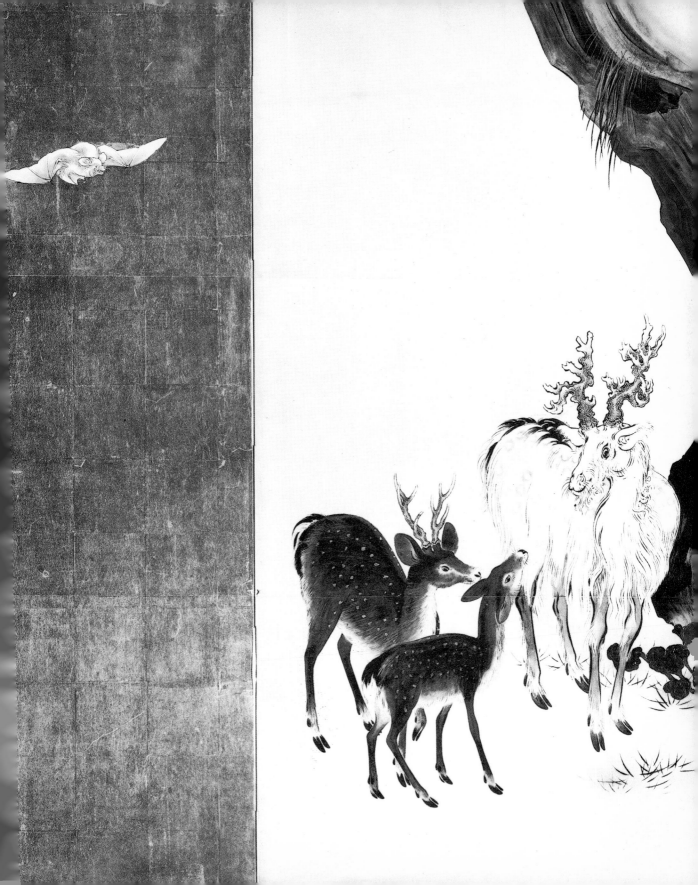

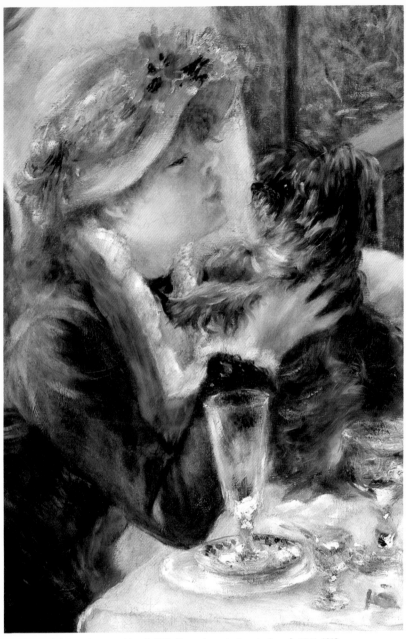

Luncheon of the Boating Party (detail), 1881. Pierre Auguste Renoir. French, 1841–1919

No artists have drawn with more simplicity and purity of line than the Persians, Chinese and Japanese. But credit goes to the artists of the West for the warmth and feeling and vivacity with which they paint. Here, Renoir makes us feel how the girl adores the dog and, in return, how blissfully happy the dog is to be adored! The pretty girl was an artist's model named Aline Charigot whom Renoir was in love with when he painted this picture, and married shortly afterwards.

A young Spanish prince named Philip Prosper also loved his dog so much that when his portrait was to be painted he very much wanted his pet to be in the picture too. The painter, Velázquez, agreed, with the result that Philip (who is not seen here) had to stand for his picture while the dog (opposite) jumped into the comfortable chair – and stole the show!

Dog (detail from *Prince Philip Prosper*). Diego Velázquez. Spanish, 1599–1660

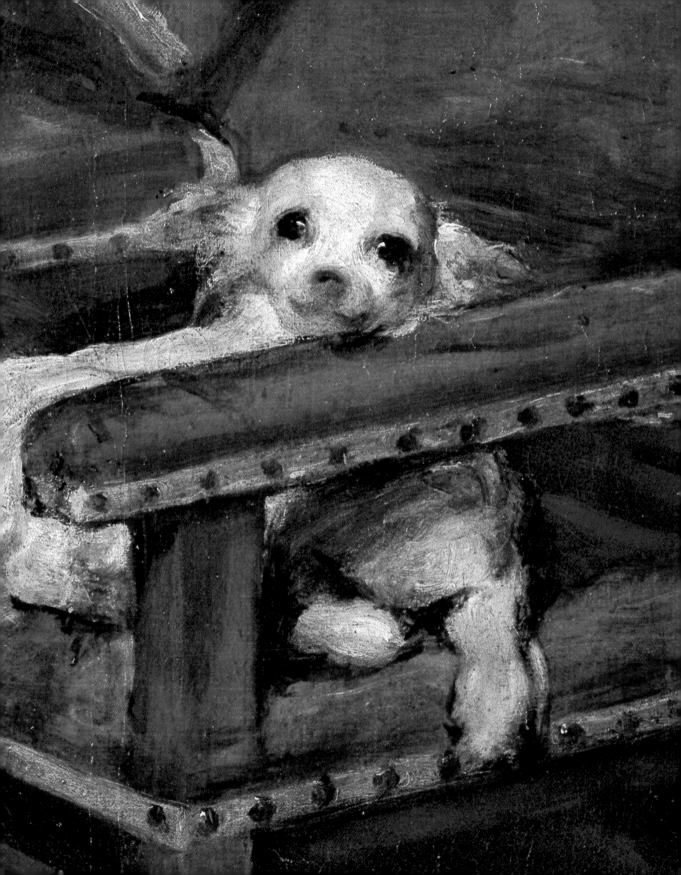

Besides serving as a subject for drawings, paintings, and pottery, animals have been popular needlework and tapestry motifs for centuries. This handsome creature prancing through the underbrush in a forest is one of several hounds in a famous tapestry depicting the hunt and capture of a unicorn.

In the modern painting at right we feel the enthusiasm and speed with which the dachshund is scurrying forward. The artist was more interested in creating the impression of continuous movement – in the dog's legs, its owner's feet, in the quick to-and-fro flick of the tail and the rhythmic swing of the leash – than he was in painting a conventional portrait of a dog.

Dog in a Thicket (detail from *The Unicorn Defends Himself*). From the *Hunt of the Unicorn* tapestries. French or Flemish, late 15th cent. From the Château de Verteuil

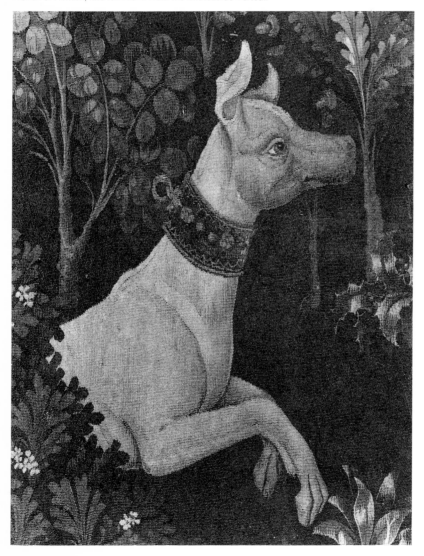

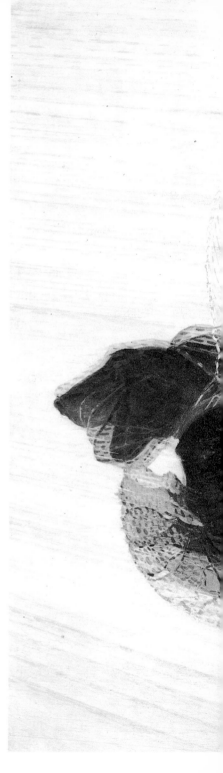

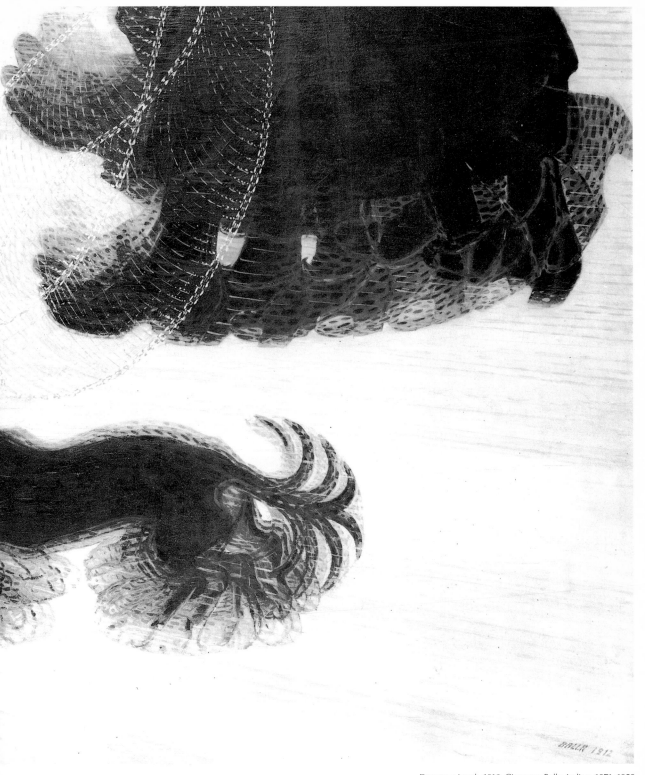

Dog on a Leash, 1912. Giacomo Balla. Italian, 1871–1958

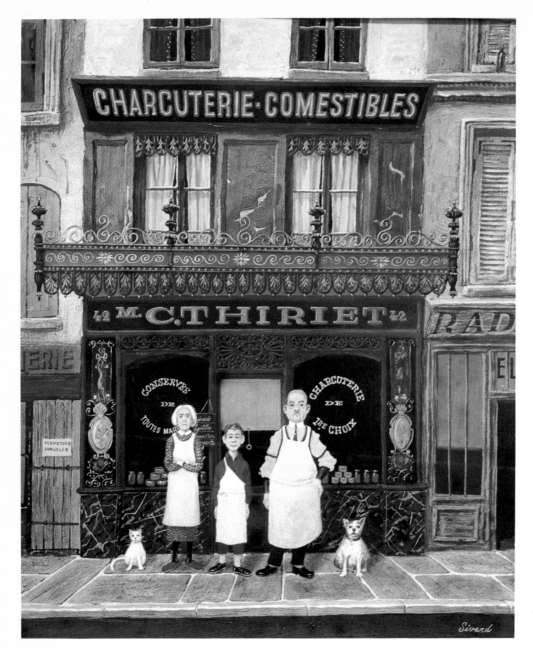

The Wool-winder.
Jean-Baptiste Greuze.
French, 1725–1805

La Charcuterie.
Robert Sivard.
American, b. 1914

This is precisely the way an artist or photographer today would normally tell a family *not* to pose for a picture – one, two, three, four, five – stiffly in a row. Yet, it's the typical old-fashioned pose, and the inclusion of the cat and the dog as equally important members of the French grocer's family, that make this painting so enormously appealing.

The pretty girl with a cat (opposite) was also painted in Paris, but over two hundred years earlier. It's not only the clothes that belong to the eighteenth century, but the charming, almost too-good-to-be-true manner in which the artist posed and painted his subject.

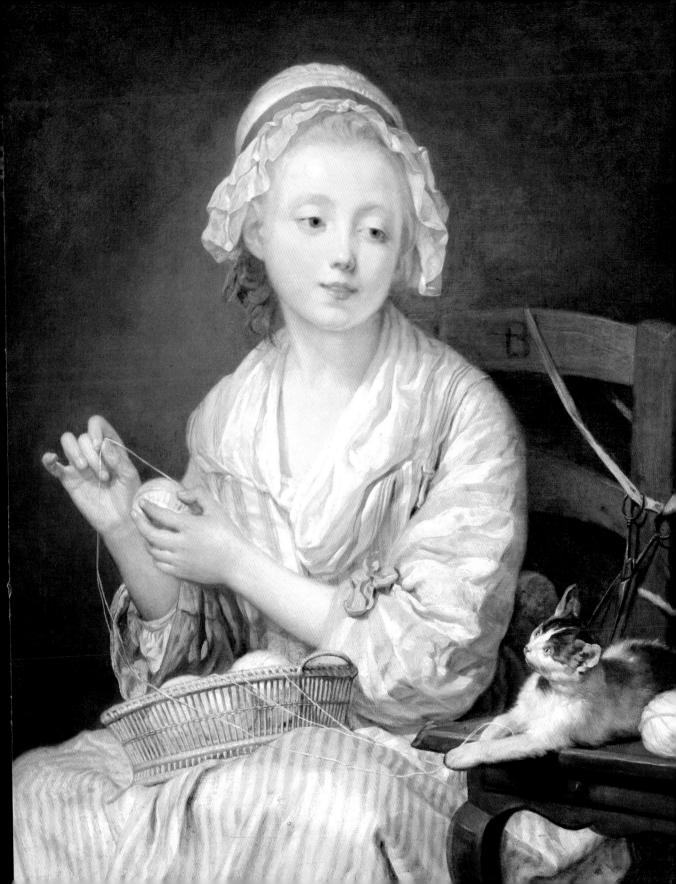

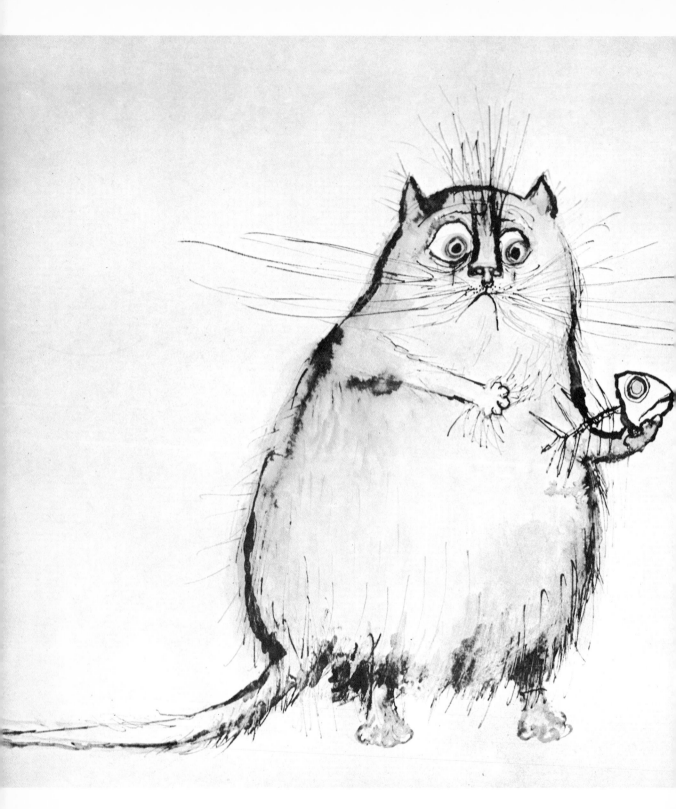

Just as the style of painting by Greuze on page 59 is typical of the eighteenth century, Ronald Searle's cat on the opposite page could only belong to the present century – and *now*. It's interesting how two utterly different kinds of studies can look equally cat-like and appealing; this modern one humorously so, the earlier one in a pretty kind of way.

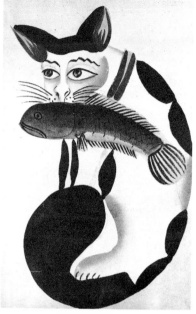

An Indian folk artist also chose the cat-with-fish theme and made the almost stencil-like design at left. The expression in the eyes is even more human – and wild – than in those of Searle's disappointed cat.

Fat Cat. Ronald Searle. English, b. 1920

Cat with Fish in its Mouth. Kalighat watercolour. Indian, c. 1890

Golden Fish. Paul Klee. Swiss, 1879–1940

A certain air of mystery and humour envelops almost everything Paul Klee ever painted. The picture below is one of several variations of what the modern Swiss master simply called 'fish magic'.

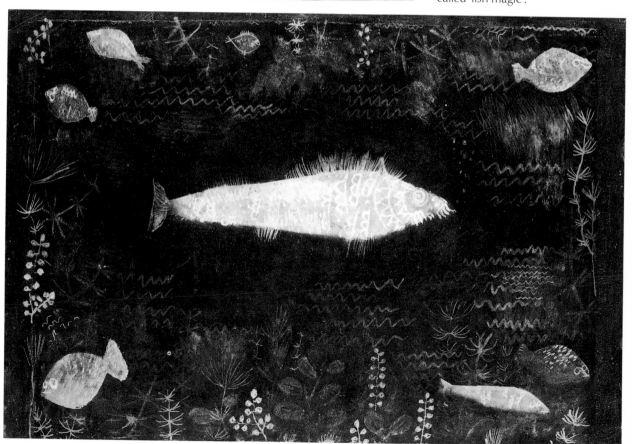

Who first thought up the idea of dressing animals like people and writing stories in which animals think, speak, and act like humans no one can really tell. But since the last century, generation after enchanted generation has been brought up on them. Sometimes it is forgotten how highly prized as works of art the best of these illustrations have become. The ones on this page, for instance, belong to two of the most distinguished museums in England.

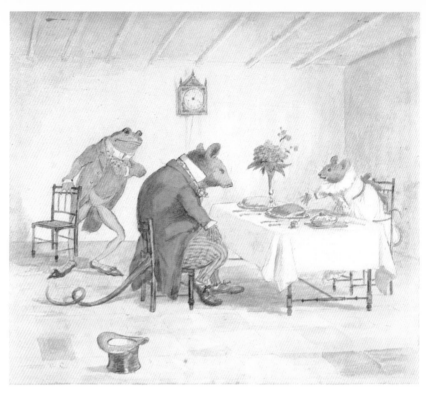

Frog he would a-wooing go.
Randolph Caldecott. English, 1846–86

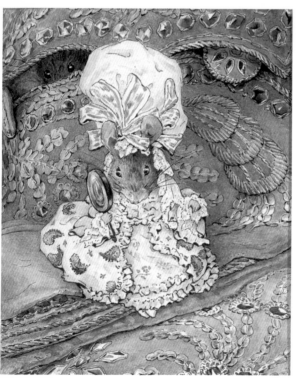

Lady Mouse in a Mob Cap. From *The Tailor of Gloucester.*
Beatrix Potter. English, 1866–1943

Randolph Caldecott was one of the first artists to make the characters in children's books look real. The 'frog who would a-wooing go', drawn in 1885, is a delightfully typical example.

Millions have grown up with Beatrix Potter's *The Tale of Peter Rabbit* and her other illustrated stories. Miss Potter was always *most* painstaking both in her research of animals and the costumes in which she dressed them, particularly 'nice little mice' like this beauty seated on the 'satin waistcoat – trimmed with gauze and green worsted chenille – for the Mayor of Gloucester'. She created this little masterpiece in 1903.

Almost completely unknown in the West, although it shouldn't be, is the wonderful harum-scarum illustration on the opposite page, which comes from an old Japanese book for children.

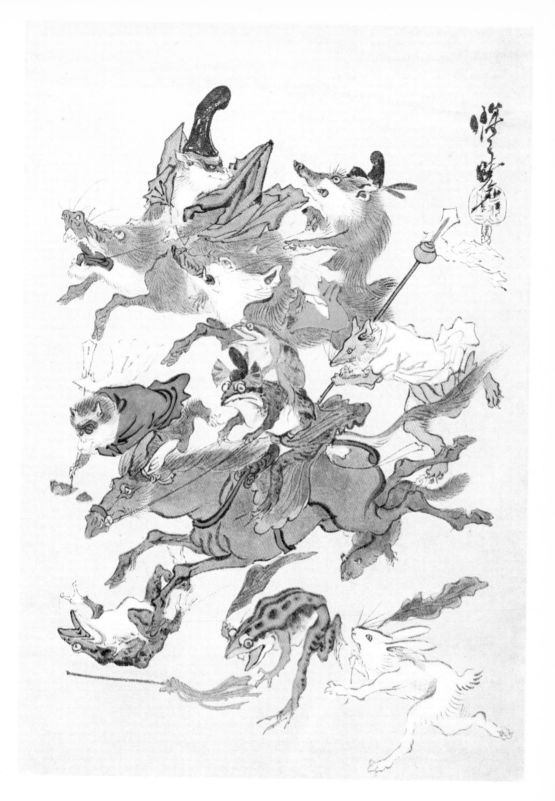

Illustration for *The Snake and the Frogs*. Kawanabe Gyosai. Japanese, 1831–99. From *The Studio*, 1899

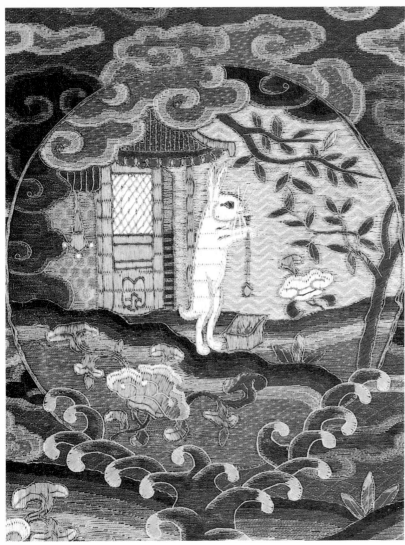

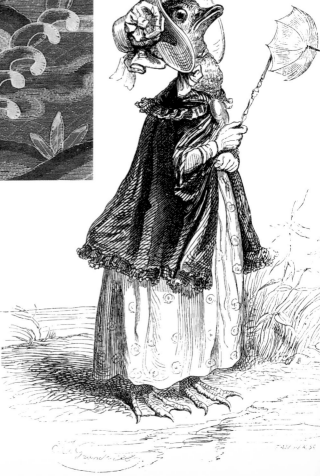

Rabbit. Embroidered silk medallion. Unknown artist.
Chinese, late 16th or early 17th cent.

At first glance, the figure above resembles the White
Rabbit in *Alice in Wonderland* as he pulled out his pocket
watch and said to himself, 'Oh dear! Oh dear! I shall be
too late!' But in fact this scene was embroidered in China
centuries before Lewis Carroll wrote *Alice*. What the
Chinese white rabbit seems to be doing is holding up a
spade with the object of digging up a plant, placing it in a
pot, and carrying it indoors to enjoy in his living-room –
which is as fanciful an idea as a white rabbit dressing up
in a coat and white kid gloves to visit a duchess – or
almost!

64

Perhaps the most lastingly popular illustrator of classic fairy tales is Arthur Rackham. Here are the three bears from the story of that name – indignant, to say the least, to discover that their house had been stolen into while they were out. 'And here she is,' screams Wee Bear at finding the culprit in *his* bed.

Inside every one of us are tendencies that are similar to animals. And because some of them are stronger in one person than in another, it is easy to understand why such clever drawings as the one at left and the one below *do* look so very much like certain people we know.

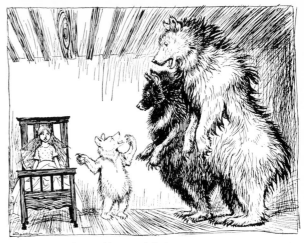

Three Bears. Arthur Rackham. English, 1867–1939

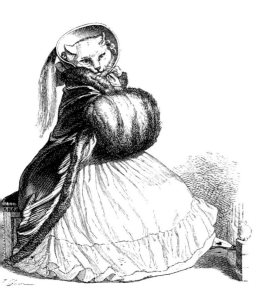

'What is it you want to buy?' This is the scene from *Through the Looking-Glass* after the White Queen has suddenly turned into a sheep. The shop she is now keeping is filled with all sorts of tempting things to buy, from hoops to jars of barley sugar and liquorice sticks. The sheep is still wearing the Queen's satin slippers, but Alice can't see them.

Alice and the Sheep. From Lewis Carroll: *Through the Looking-glass and What Alice Found There*, 1869. Sir John Tenniel. English, 1820–1914

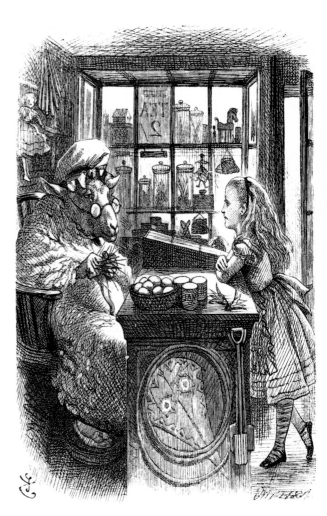

65

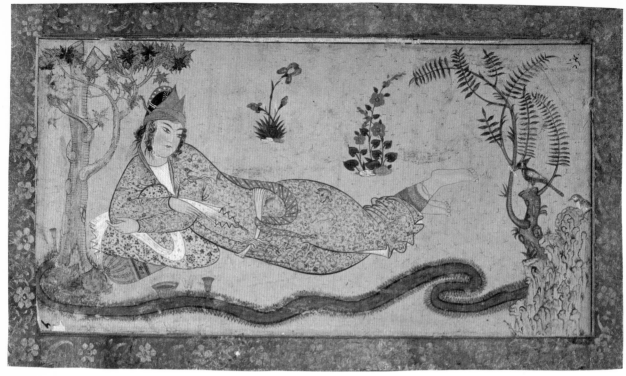

The Queen of Sheba. Unknown artist. Persian, c.1600

Besides history, people, legends, fantasy and animals, another whole area of enchantment lies in the land itself – in the fields and woodlands, and especially in the garden.

Around his house or castle, even around the humblest hut, man has lent nature a helping hand. By rooting out weeds and cultivating the soil he has raised food to eat, and planted trees, shrubs and flowers to enjoy for their beauty.

The well-planned garden, man's 'dream kingdom', is the kind of earthly paradise poets have written odes to, where artists have always loved to paint, and Romeos to meet their Juliets.

Above is how a sixteenth-century Persian artist envisioned the famous queen who journeyed to meet King Solomon. Obviously the artist believed the Queen of Sheba to be just as beautiful as the Bible tells us King Solomon was wise – and so fond of herbs and flowers that he decided to paint her in a garden.

In matters of art, as in most things, the Romans copied the Greeks. And it happens that one of the earliest existing evidences of a European garden is to be found in the ancient Roman wall painting on the opposite page. The flower that the lady, dressed in Greek fashion, is pinching off its stem has been identified as the asphodel which grew in Paradise, and which Homer refers to in his lines:

And Rest at Last where Souls
    Unlockèd Dwell
In Everlasting Meads of Asphodel.

Girl gathering Flowers. Wall painting from Stabiae. Roman, 1st cent. AD

Overleaf: *Versailles, View of the Palace and Gardens in 1668.* Pierre Patel. French, c.1605–76

Overleaf: On the next two pages is an early view of the largest and most extravagantly conceived palace and gardens that France and perhaps the entire world had ever known. Although the Sun King, as Louis XIV was called, was most unpopular for spending such huge fortunes on the building of Versailles, this magnificent royal residence became a wonder of the seventeenth-century world. And so it remains to this day, when, fortunately, everyone who wants to go and marvel at it can do so.

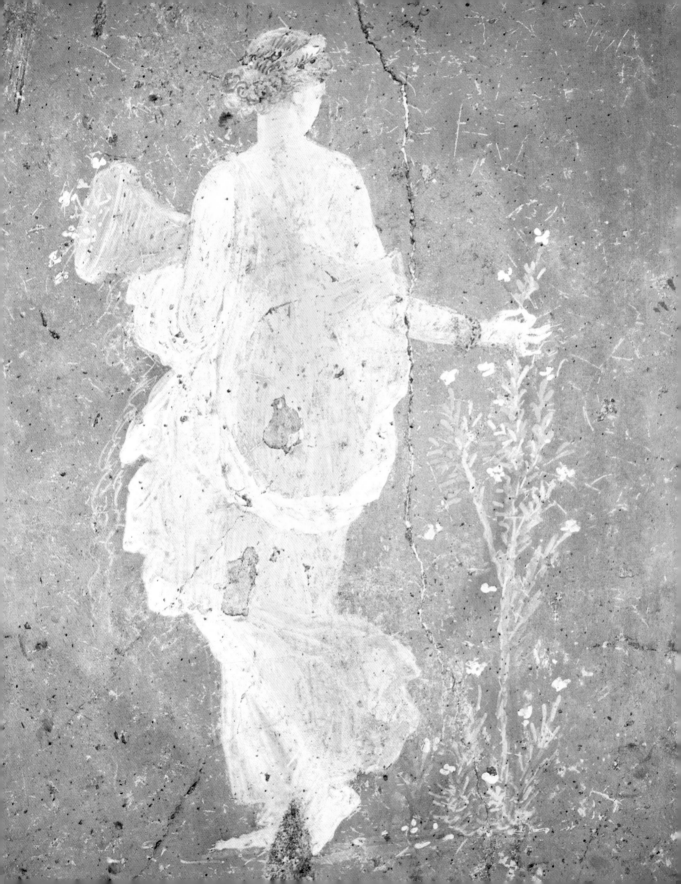

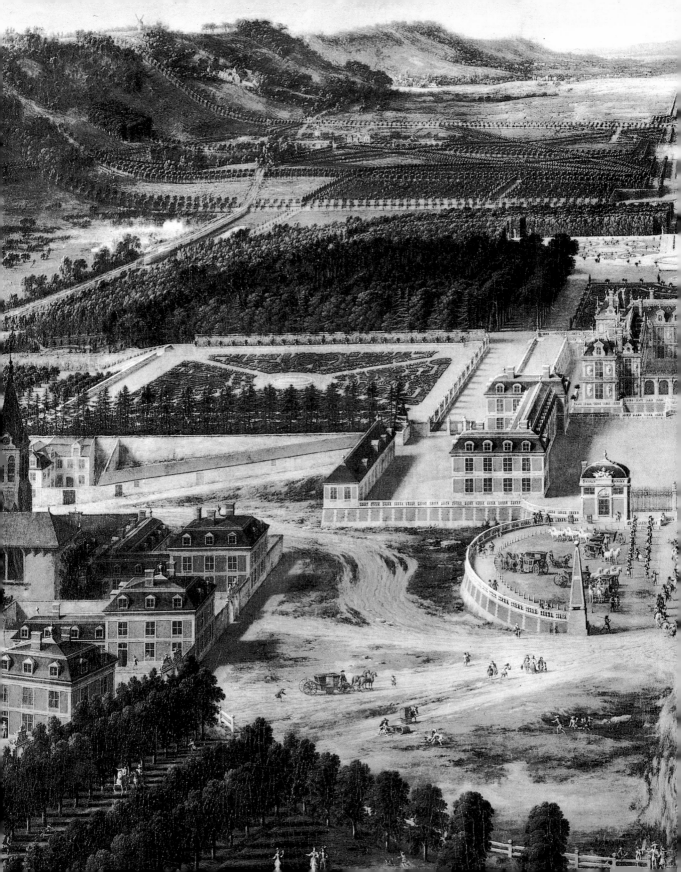

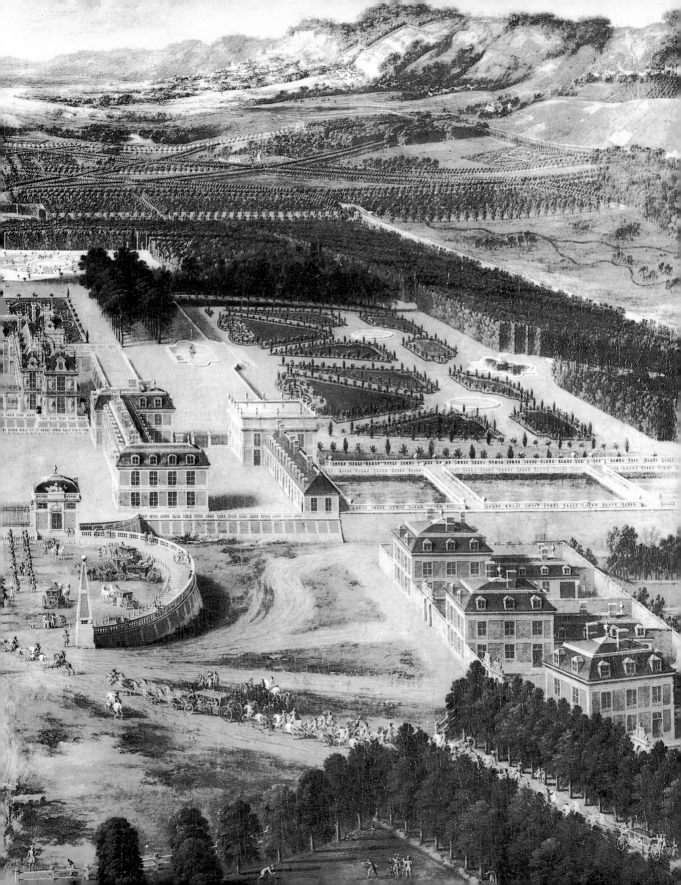

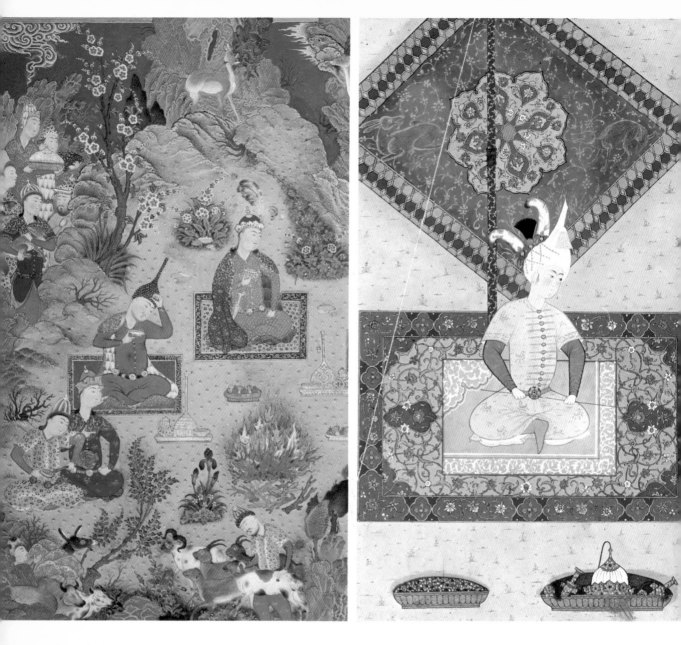

Zal Consults the Magi; Kay Khosrow's War Prizes are Pledged For; Zahhak is Told His Fate; Feast of Sadeh. From manuscript of Firdowsi: *Shahnameh (Book of Kings).* Attributed to Aqa Miraq (2nd picture from left), Sultan Muhammad (other pictures). Persian, 16th cent.

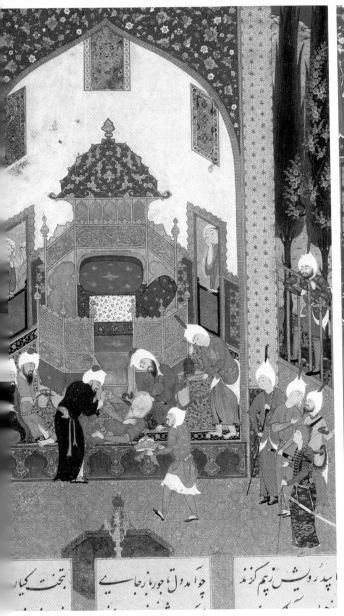

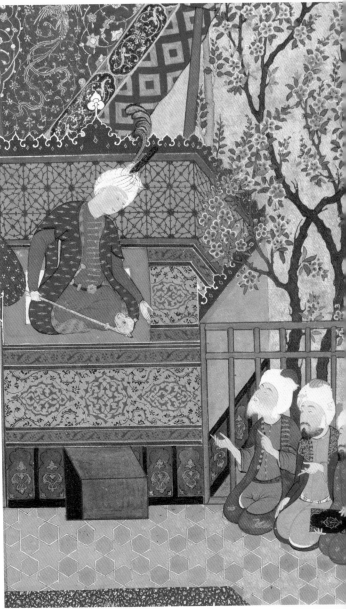

In Persia, even the princely gardens of long ago were much smaller than the average European garden, because it was hot in that country and rain was infrequent. So instead of lawns and big flower beds, the Persians made the most of courtyards, pavilions, carpets and coloured tiles. They planted flowers in small borders and in pots or urns. And, often, when they dressed up and sat in the courtyards, they looked every bit as colourful as the flowers themselves.

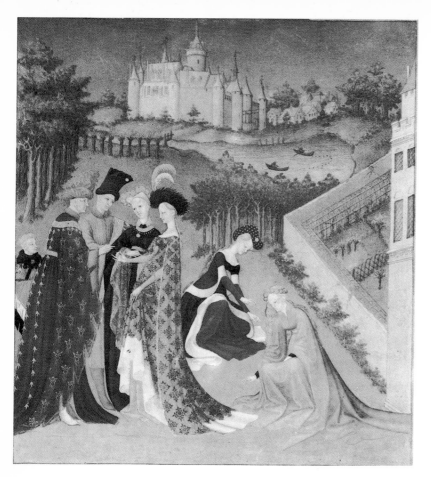

In these days of jeans, it's hard to believe that once upon a time people really did dress as elegantly as the party above – and in the daytime, too! The picture represents April in a series of twelve miniature paintings, one for each month of the year.

April. From manuscript of *Les Très Riches Heures de Jean, duc de Berry.* Pol, Jean and Herman de Limbourg. French, 15th cent.

A romantic setting for music, song – and the holding of hands – is the fifteenth-century 'pleasure garden' opposite with its shady trees, gay borders of flowers, and a splashing fountain in the middle of the lawn.

Lovers in Garden. From manuscript of *Le Roman de la rose.* French, 15th cent.

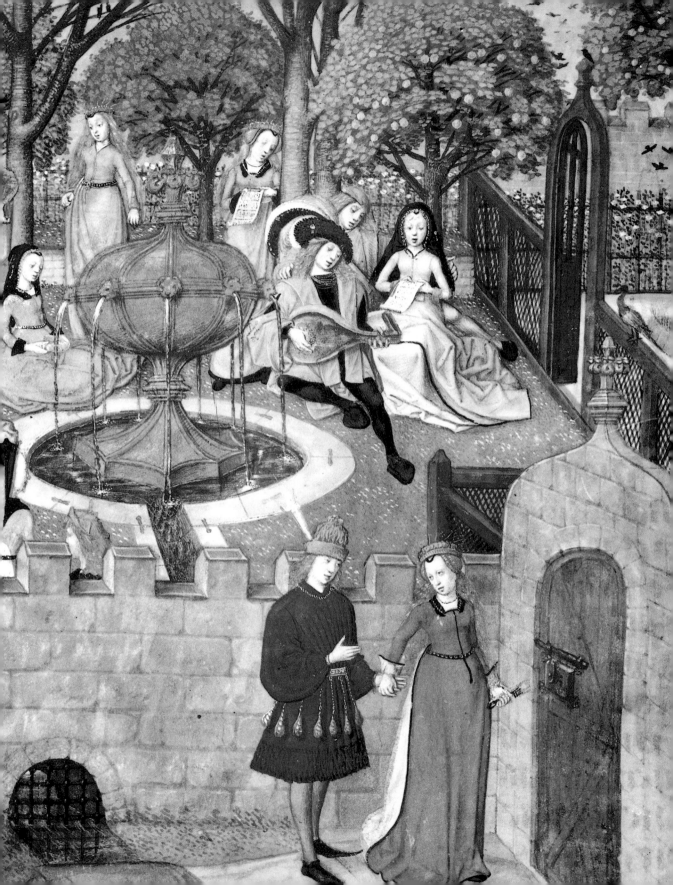

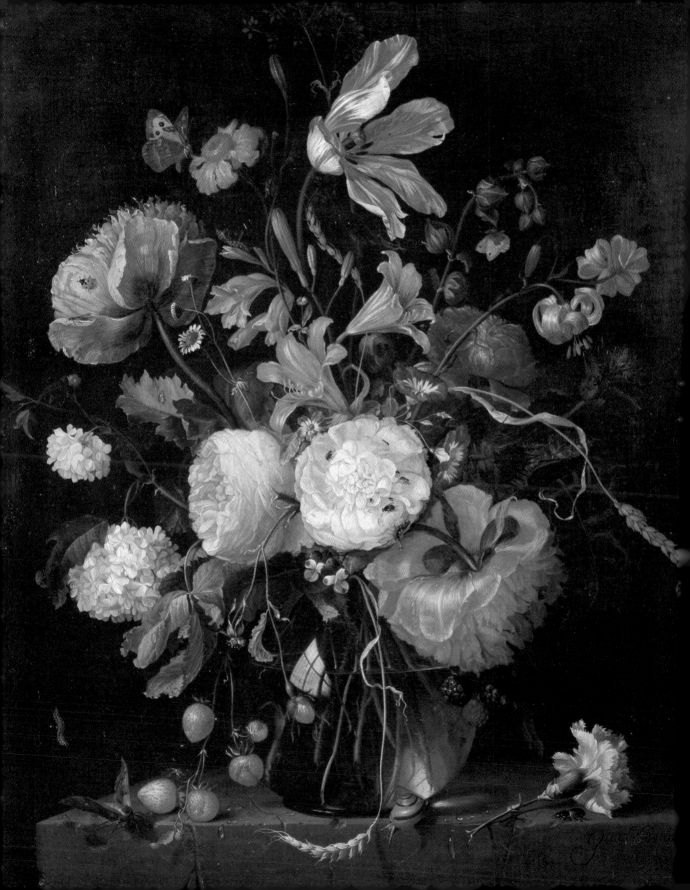

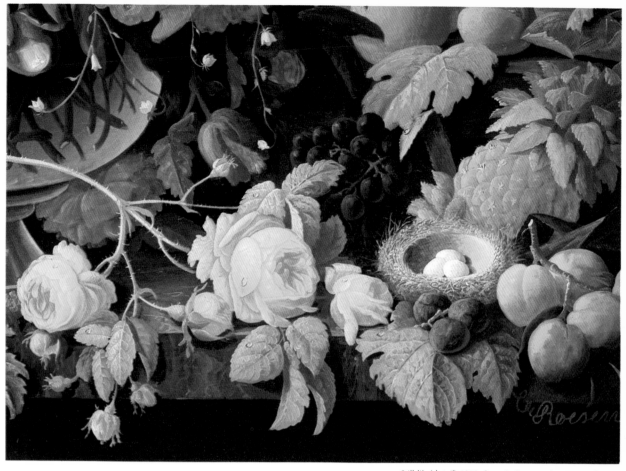

The gardener's joy in cultivating flowers is matched by a lady's delight in cutting them to arrange indoors, and the artist's desire to paint them. The fullness of the still-life opposite, and the artist's patient attention to the smallest of details – those tiny little insects clinging to the petals, for instance – are part of the seventeenth-century Dutch tradition of flower painting.

The picture above is a detail from a nineteenth-century still-life. The American artist who did it was obviously strongly influenced by the earlier Dutch flower painters, yet his style belongs to a later era when the colours used became stronger, the outlines softer and the smaller details less meticulously worked out.

Flowers in a Glass Vase. Jacob van Walscapelle. Dutch, 1644–1727

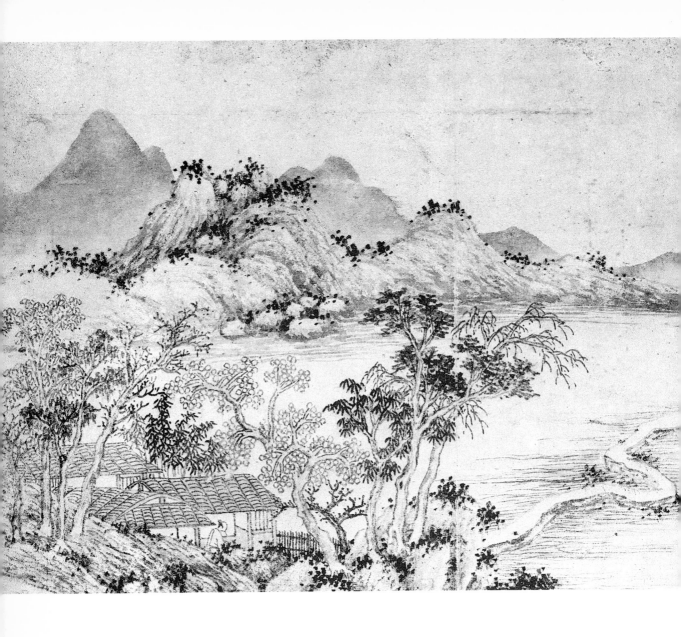

Landscape. Shen Chou. Chinese, 1427–1509

One quick glance tells us that no European or American artist could have painted these landscapes. But it's harder to recognize the difference between a Chinese painting, as above, and a Japanese painting, as at right. The Japanese have usually painted with stronger outlines and colours. Here the artist has concentrated on the bird and its immediate surroundings, allowing the distance to fade into the mist. In the Chinese painting, which is a more complete panorama, the artist catches our imagination by drawing us in to keep looking further and further into the distance.

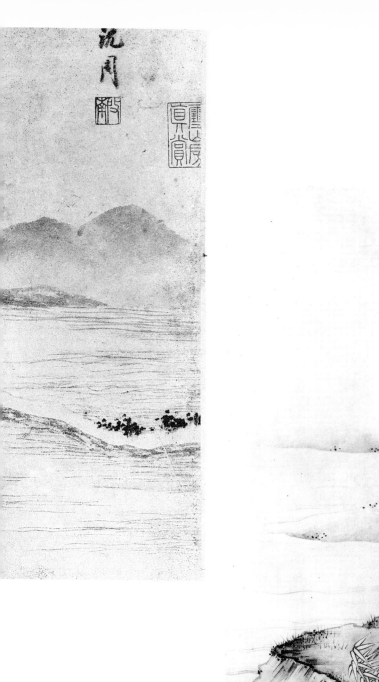

Flowers and Birds in a Spring Landscape.
Attributed to Kano Motonobu.
Japanese, 1476–1559

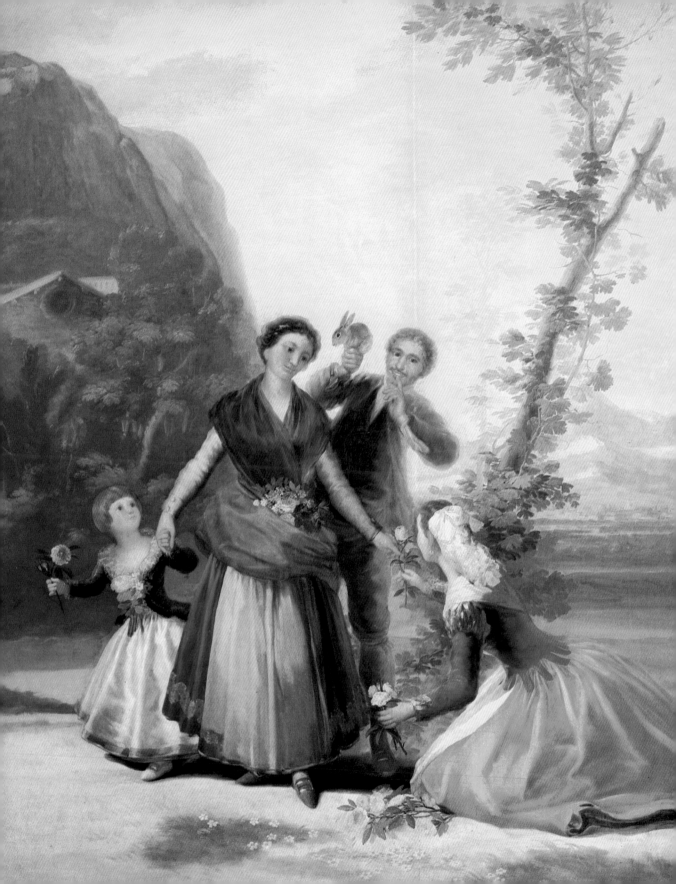

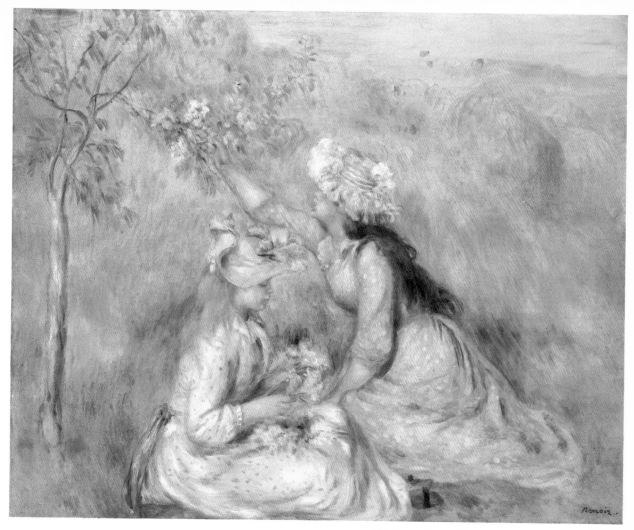

Girls Picking Flowers. Pierre-Auguste Renoir. French, 1841–1919.

In the sparkling scene opposite, Goya has used flowers as a symbol of springtime, youth, and the enjoyment of life. Everything in the picture is fresh, colourful, and unexpected, including the rabbit which the man is playfully holding up in the air, ready to surprise the lady and the child holding hands.

The Flower Women. Francisco de Goya. Spanish, 1746–1828

Sunlight brings colour to everything it touches, as opposed to moonlight in which everything is reduced to shades of grey. In this oil painting the artist has arranged his colours so vibratingly that the whole canvas sings with life. We can feel the warmth of the sunny spring day, the coolness of the fresh green grass, and we can all but smell the blossoms that the girls are gathering.

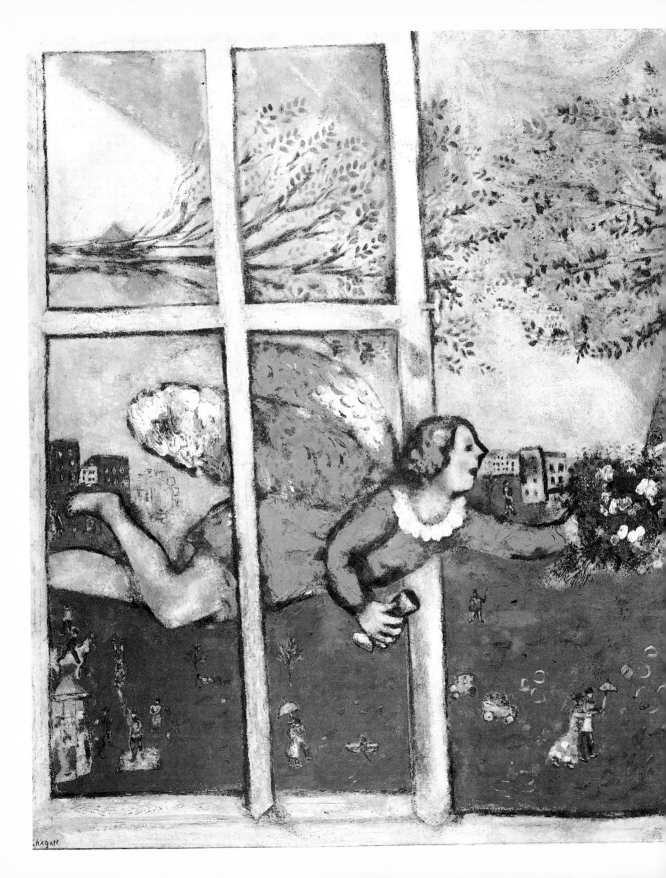

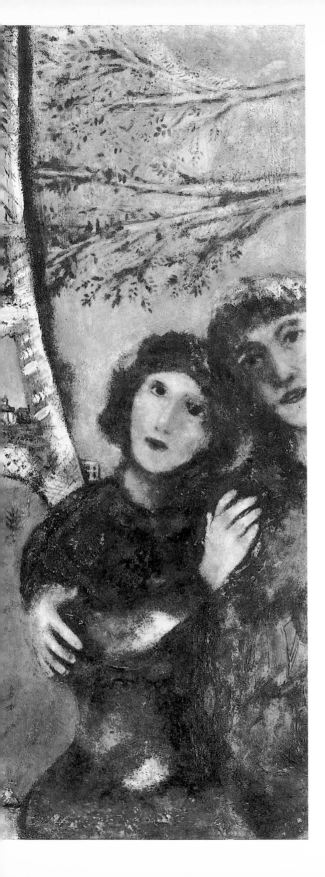

Here is the way two of the greatest artists of our own century have 'said it with flowers'. Chagall's picture (at left) is as different from Picasso's (below) as both are from anything we have seen earlier.

After he had left Russia, Chagall fell so head over heels in love with Paris, and with life in general, that he painted one scene after another like this. His floating images, his lovers, and his flowers tell the world how light-hearted and happy he felt. 'When you have love, you work', he once said.

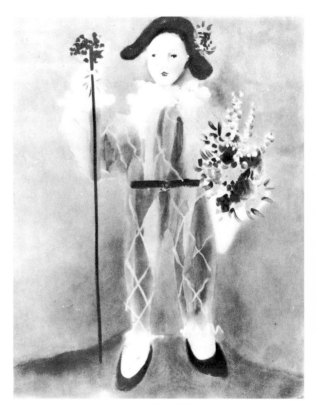

Harlequin. Pablo Picasso. Spanish, 1881–1973

Picasso was also fond of flowers, but rarely is there even the suggestion of a bouquet in his paintings – nor anything more charming than the lovely example above.

Homage to the Eiffel Tower, 1928. Marc Chagall. Russian, b.1887

Enchantment also lies in pageantry and entertainment; in colourful processions and ceremonies, in fêtes and firework displays, in the magic that enfolds as the lights go up at the theatre, ballet, or opera.

The splendid painting at right shows England's first Queen Elizabeth being transported in a stately procession toward Blackfriars. In those days, such an occasion would have been missed by all but a few. On special occasions *these* days, all the world has to do to get a close-up view of England's second Queen Elizabeth in glittering regal attire – and in a coach of gold too, sometimes – is to flick on the switch and remain glued to a television set.

What a painter can do and a camera can't do is to detach the main characters and reorganize things in such a way that all sorts of subtle movements, interesting expressions and amusing details – such as the gesture here of the sauntering bearer of the Great Sword of State with his hand on his hip – are contained in a single picture that we can enjoy going over again and again.

Overleaf: One of the world's greatest showplaces is the ancient city of Venice, where glittering palaces rise out of the sea. The artists who most often painted this dream city of canals and gondolas and regattas were Guardi and Canaletto, the latter in the most glowing colours and on the most festive, crowded, and sunny occasions. A traditional celebration was the 'marriage of Venice to the Adriatic' – the Adriatic being the sea which still laps at the city's steps.

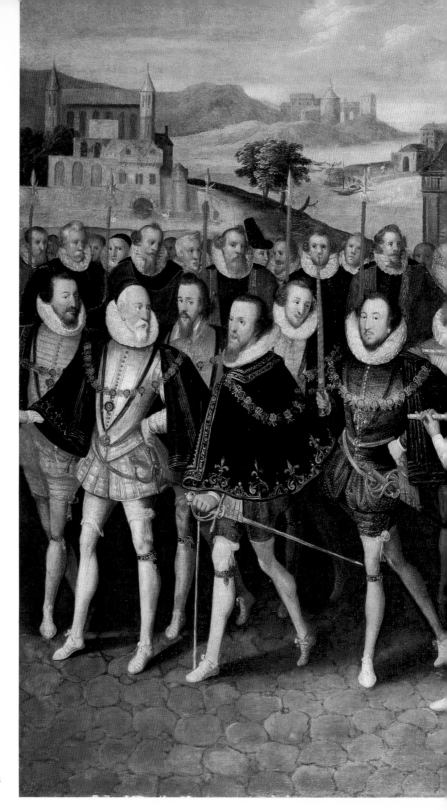

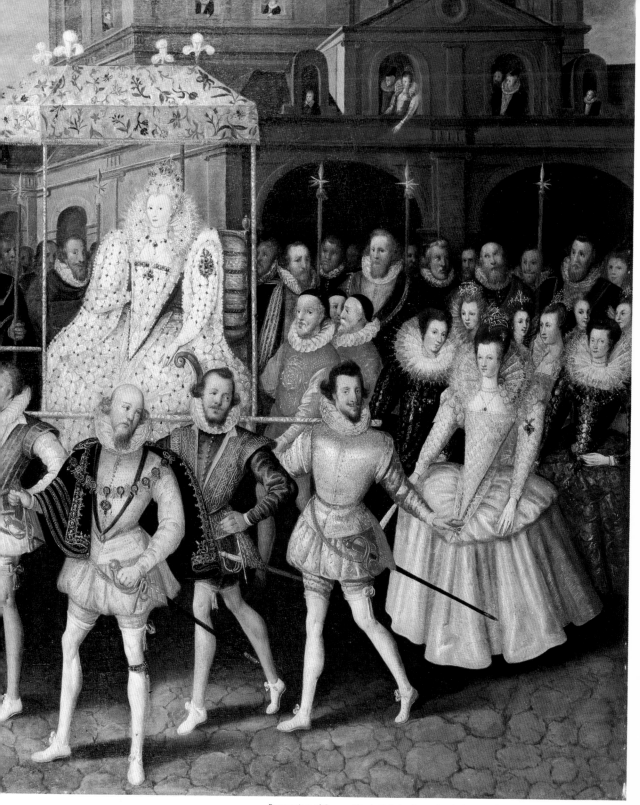

Procession of Queen Elizabeth I. Attributed to Robert Peake the Elder. English, c.1580–1626

Overleaf: *Marriage of Venice to the Adriatic*. Canaletto (Giovanni Antonio Canal). Italian, 1697–1768

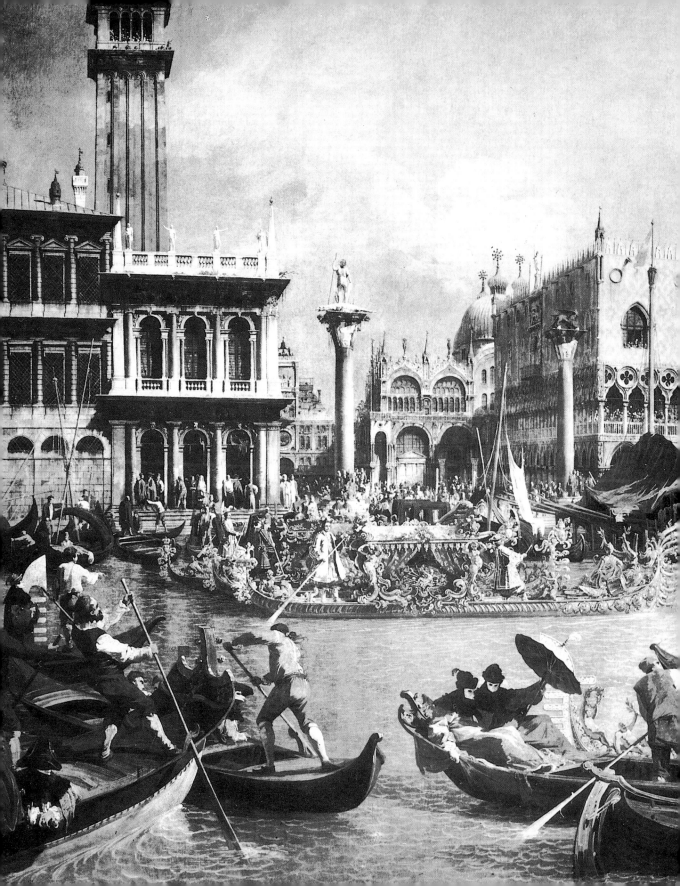

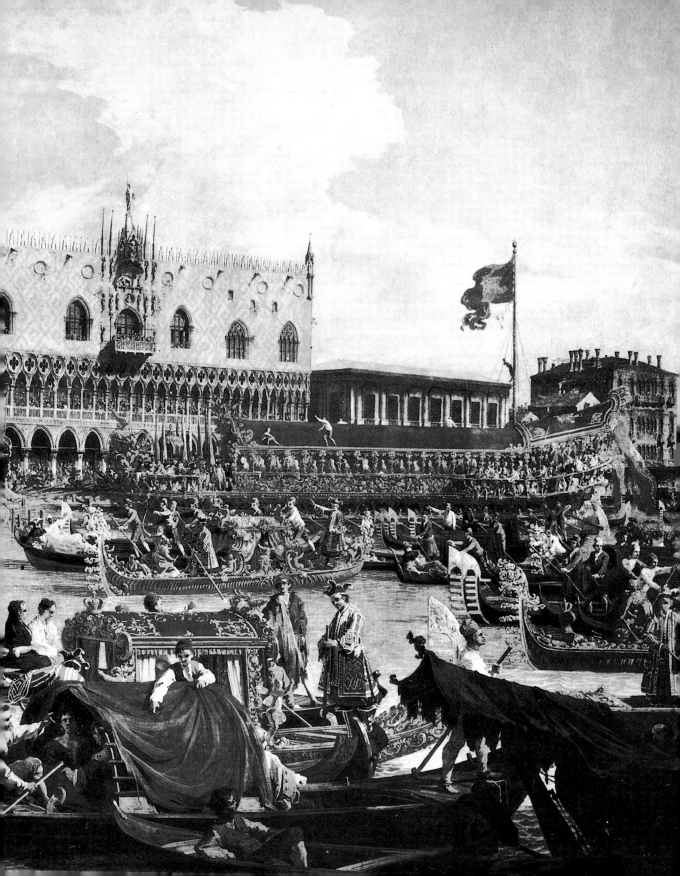

For sheer enchantment it would be hard to find a more dreamlike scene than this vast, stage-like setting by Fragonard, the French artist who flourished at the court of King Louis XVI, immortalizing the whims and never-never land fantasies of the Queen, Marie-Antoinette. Contributing to the aura of magic are the bursts of sunlight that touch the bank and the pleasure boat and crown the long line of trees with gold.

Fête at Rambouillet. Jean-Honoré Fragonard. French, 1732–1806

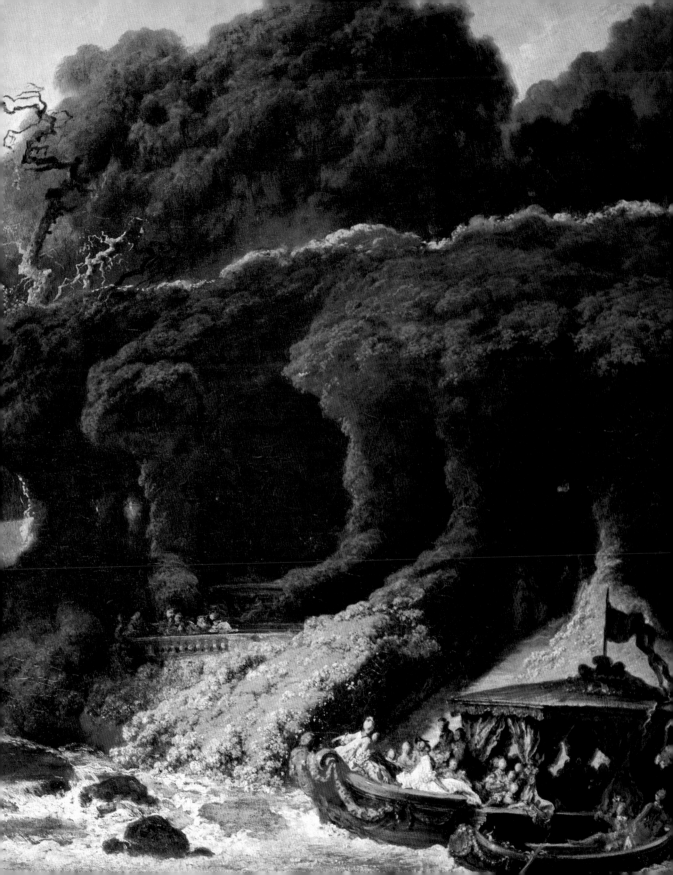

For those who enjoyed showing off a pretty dress – or a dashing figure – Vauxhall Gardens was once *the* place to go. And as for chatterboxes, the concerts seemed far less important than the chance to gossip! While painting this fashionable haunt near London in 1781, Rowlandson, who never hesitated to exaggerate a face, a figure, or an idea to make a picture more amusing, included noted personalities of the day – and many more of them than could ever have been on hand at one time. Toward the right, for instance, he squeezed in the Prince of Wales (later King George IV), whispering in the ear of Perdita Robinson, the pretty young lady in white.

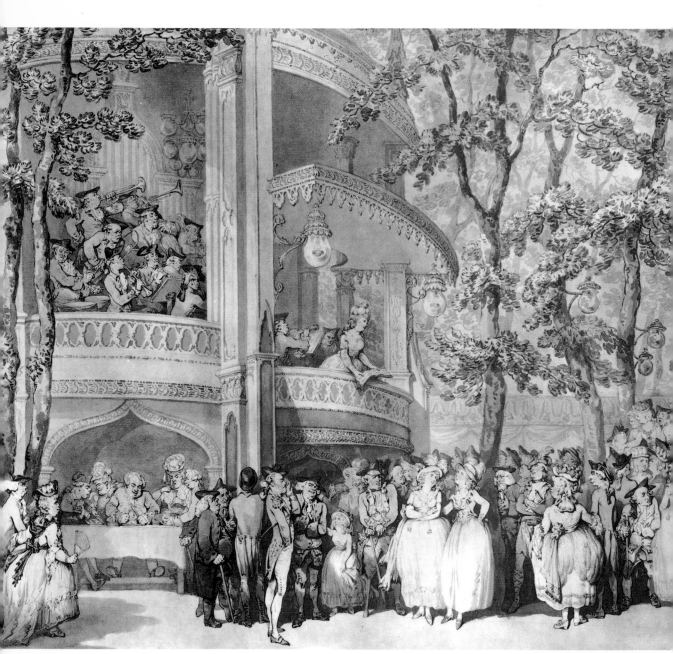

Vauxhall Gardens. Thomas Rowlandson. English, 1756–1827

At a fancy dress ball, can anyone be sure who, or even what, he may find himself dancing with – a princess, a frog, a witch, or an enchanting carnation such as Grandville drew at right . . . with a caterpillar nibbling at the ribbon on her gown?

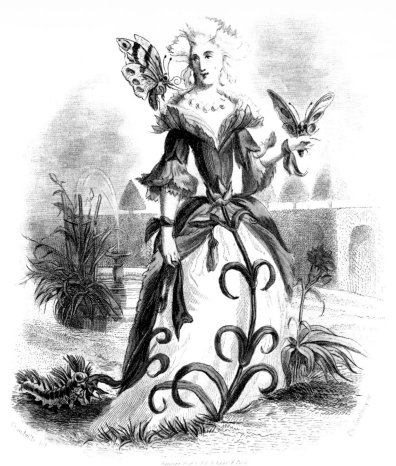

Carnation. From *Les Fleurs animeés.* J. I. Grandville. French, 1803–47

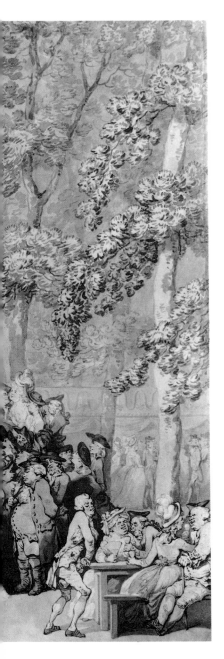

Fireworks. Anonymous English watercolour design, 1813.

Ever since gunpowder was invented, some people have been willing to set guns aside – for an evening at least – in favour of a firework display. This elegant one went off in 1813 to celebrate the engagement of Princess Charlotte Augusta, the daughter of the Prince of Wales, to Prince William of Orange. However, after more fireworks, the engagement was broken off.

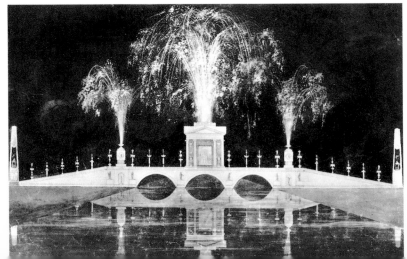

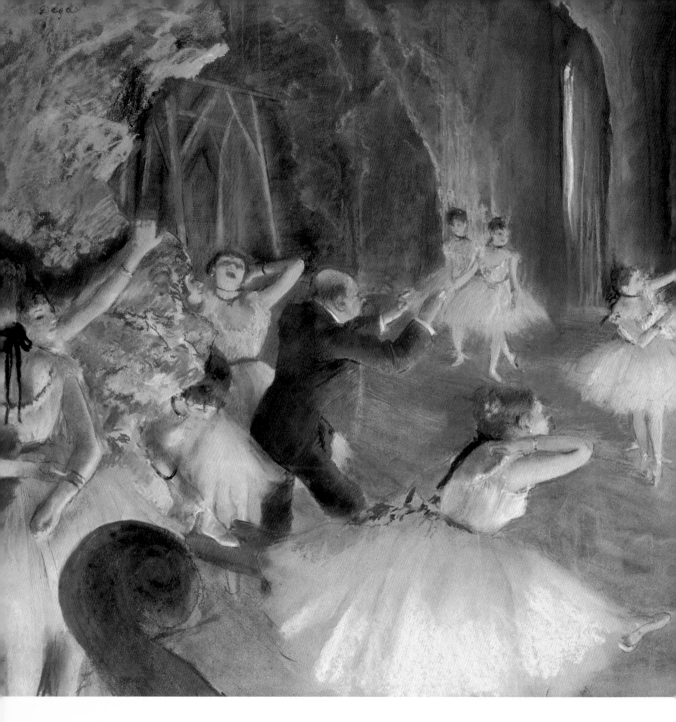

Not only is the beauty of the human body most poetically displayed by dancers, but they are trained to express every kind of thought and emotion by a movement or gesture; never in words. No artist has done more to popularize ballet than the French artist Degas. And during rehearsals, which he often went to, if a dancer stopped to yawn or scratch her back or lean against a piece of scenery, Degas managed to make it all part of the magic.

90

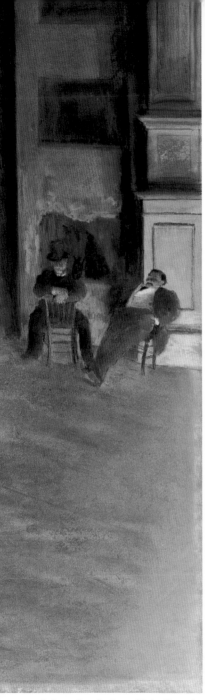

Rehearsal on the Stage. Hilaire-Germain-Edgar Degas. French, 1834–1917

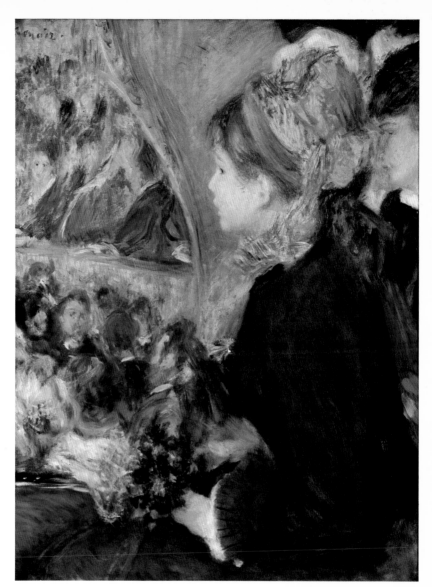

The Cabaret. Pierre-Auguste Renoir. French, 1841–1919

The wonder and inner excitement of a girl's first outing at the theatre is revealed very subtly here by her expression. The importance of the occasion is further emphasized by her pretty dress and hat, chosen and put on with such obvious care. The painting is also perfectly composed. While almost evenly dividing the couple from the rest of the audience, the plain background of the side of the box allows the girl's face to stand out clearly, while the direction in which her main interest lies – toward the stage beyond the limits of the picture – keeps returning our eyes to the left.

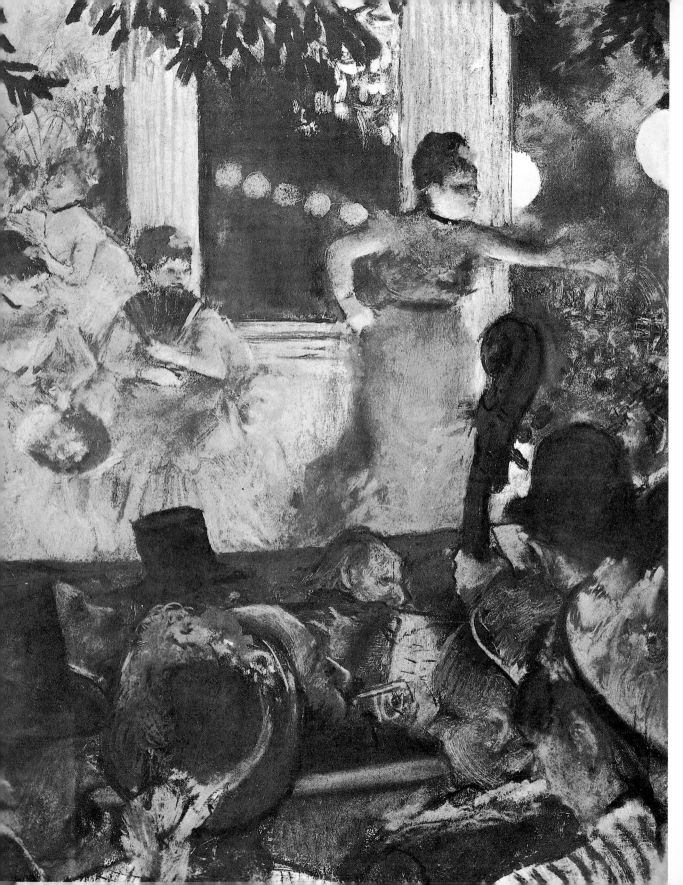

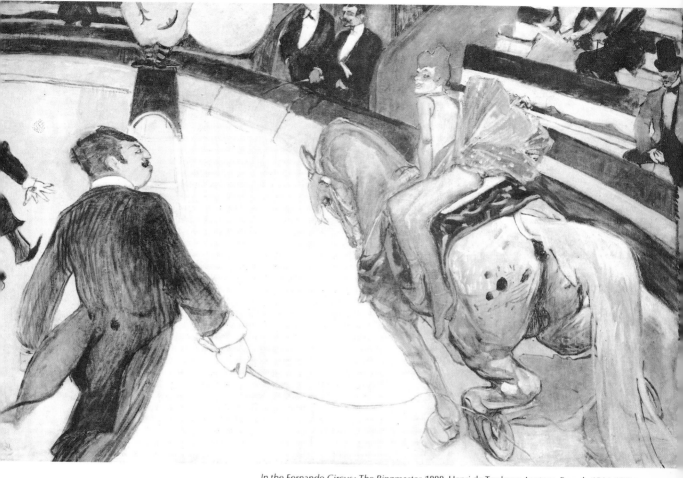

In the Fernando Circus: The Ringmaster, 1888. Henri de Toulouse-Lautrec. French, 1864–1901

From the late 1870s through the so-called 'gay nineties', Paris enjoyed a period of general prosperity and kicking up of heels. Cafés, cabarets, and concerts – as in Degas' picture opposite – were as popular as champagne. So was the sparkling Fernando Circus which Toulouse Lautrec visited over and over again – and painted, as above.

The 1870s were also marked by a group of artists – Monet, Degas, Renoir, among them – who struggled hard for their new way of painting to find favour with the critics and the public. Photography was well established, and in freeing themselves from the smooth and detailed 'photographic' way of painting – and from the

predominant use of browns and greys – the Impressionists, as they called themselves, went all out for light, bright and cheerful atmospheric effects. But it wasn't until our own century that the world began to appreciate what a great contribution to art the Impressionists had made.

Orange and Red on Red, 1957. Mark Rothko. American, 1903–70

As the rebellion against photographic realism was renewed in the twentieth century, the biggest excitement was the arrival of abstract painting. Here colour, pattern and texture became, essentially, the whole story a picture told. Why, necessarily, hang a conventional painting on the wall, it was asked, when arrangements of colour and line (as in these handsome compositions by Mark Rothko and Kenneth Noland) can

bring so much satisfaction too? Shapes and colours can create a mood that draws us into an imaginary space – an enchanted world of their own.

A modern American artist who knew all about enchantment was Alexander Calder, the inventor of mobiles, stabiles, and many, many other things. He also knew as nobody else did how to twist a simple piece of wire, add a few frills and produce a masterpiece like the one on the opposite page. The lion is part of a whole circus which is just one of the hundreds of wonderfully different things Calder spent his life creating.

Transwest. Kenneth Noland. American, b. 1924

94

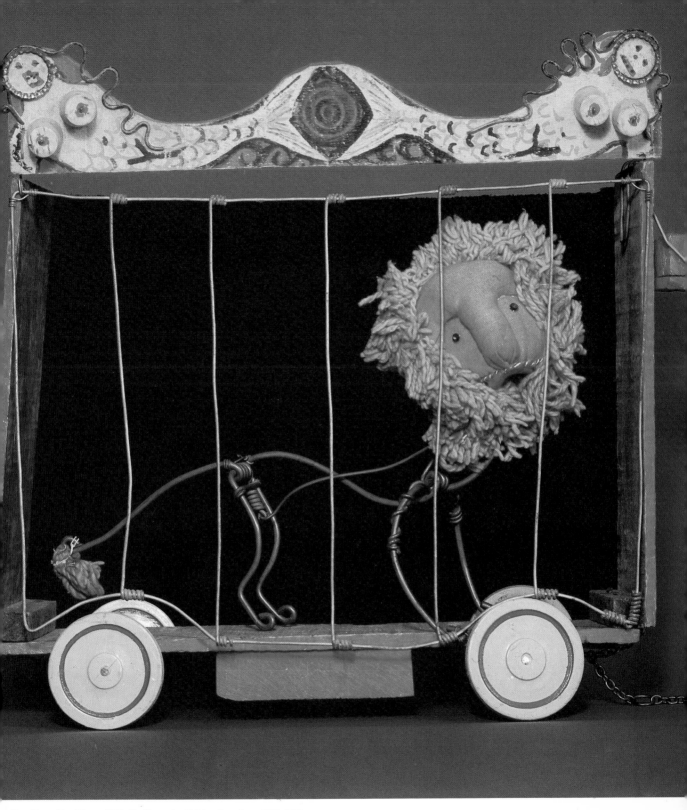

Lion. From *The Circus*, 1926–31. Alexander Calder. American, 1898–1976

ARTISTS AND ILLUSTRATIONS